The Endless Fountain

All lovely tales that we have heard or read;
An endless fountain of immortal drink,
Pouring unto us from the heaven's brink.
Nor do we merely feel these essences
For one short hour; . . . .
They must be always with us, or we die.

John Keats, *Endymion*

The Endless Fountain
Essays on Classical Humanism

Edited by Mark Morford

Ohio State University Press: Columbus

Library of Congress Cataloging in Publication Data
Main entry under title:

The Endless fountain.

  Papers presented at a symposium in honor of C. A.
Forbes held at Ohio State University, Mar. 12–13, 1971.
  1. Classical literature—Addresses, essays,
lectures. I. Forbes, Clarence Allen, 1901–
II. Morford, Mark, 1929–   ed.
PA26.F6   809   79–188742
ISBN 0–8142–0173–3

for

Clarence Allen Forbes

Contents

	Preface	ix
	Foreword *by Mark Morford*	xi
I	*Charles L. Babcock* The Classics and the New Humanism	3
II	*William F. McDonald* Classicism, Christianity, and Humanism	28
III	*David F. Heimann* Christian Humanism in the Fourth Century: Saint Jerome	58
IV	*Oskar Seidlin* Goethe's *Iphigenia in Tauris:* A Modern Use of a Greek Dramatic Theme	127
V	*Harry C. Rutledge* Classical Latin Poetry: An Art for Our Time	136
	Epilogue *by Kenneth M. Abbott*	169
	Notes on the Contributors	173
	Index	175

Preface

In June, 1971, Professor Clarence Allen Forbes retired from the professorship of classics at the Ohio State University after more than fifty years of teaching classical subjects. In his honor a symposium was held at the university on March 12 and 13, 1971, at which the papers gathered in this book were first presented; the contributors are colleagues, friends, and students of Professor Forbes, and their differing professional affiliations and approaches to the classics are in some measure an index of the wide range of Professor Forbes's own intellectual achievements. His record as a scholar may be gauged from the bibliography of his works; but in honoring him we chose to turn to his achievement as a teacher, who with learning and modesty brought alive classical literatures and cultures for generations of students.

The symposium owed its inception to the vision and encouragement of Professor Charles Babcock, who at the time of its planning was dean of the College of Humanities. We also acknowledge with gratitude the help and support of many of Professor Forbes's colleagues and friends; and special thanks are owed to Mr. Weldon A. Kefauver, director of the Ohio State University Press. Finally, a tribute may here be paid to Mrs. Clarence Forbes, who for half a century has supported and inspired her husband, and on the occasion of the symposium participated at his side. To them both we offer this book in happiness and gratitude.

by Mark Morford

Foreword

Lass den Anfang mit dem Ende
Sich in Eins zusammenziehn!
Schneller als die Gegenstande
Selber dich vorüberfliehen!
Danke, dass die Gunst der Musen
Unvergängliches verheisst,
Den Gehalt in deinem Busen
*Und die Form in deinem Geist.**

Goethe, *Dauer im Wechsel*

In honoring Clarence Forbes, we honor a teacher and
scholar who exemplifies the timeless integrity that
Goethe's poem describes. We honor a humanist whose
life is inspired by a vision of objective verities, yet one
who is humble enough to continue the never-ending
search for Truth, so that his grasp of the "Form in his
soul" becomes an instrument of motion and change. Few
men of intellectual stature have the dynamic quality that
"unites the beginning with the end"; for many Truth is
clear and immutable, and their attitudes cannot be

---

* "Let the beginning unite with the end; let yourself fly by
more quickly than the objects; be thankful that the Muses in
their goodness promise what cannot perish—the values in your
breast and the Form in your soul."

xi

changed. Others are rootless searchers, changeable and superficial. Only among the few who can know and yet inquire will be found the great teachers.

It is tempting, in preparing a festschrift, to gather together a miscellaneous assemblage of contributions from the many friends, colleagues, and students of the recipient. Such a book would be impressive in its broad display of humanism, but it would have little unity. We have chosen rather to limit our scope and, in a brief compass, to consider the permanence of the classical humanities through the vicissitudes of nearly two thousand years of alternating decline and renaissance. Our approach is to some extent eclectic, inevitably, if we consider the range of our subject. Thus we have concentrated on but three periods of history (the fourth, the eighteenth, and the twentieth centuries), each representing a crucial stage for the classical tradition. Three of our contributions are written from a twentieth-century viewpoint, and in Professor McDonald's chapter we have the retrospective sweep of the historian to balance the more strictly contemporary perspectives of Professors Babcock and Rutledge. Whether we should share the optimism of the latter or should agree with Professor McDonald in his regret for the passing of the classical tradition, only time will show; that such a difference in attitudes is even possible argues, at least, against an ossified tradition and indicates a certain vitality in contemporary classicism. There will be less room for argument about the two periods of the past that we have considered here. Professor Seidlin shows us how "the intelligible forms of ancient poets" (the phrase is Coleridge's) inspired German literary genius at the end of the eighteenth century, and in so doing he speaks eloquently for the benign influence of the classics upon the German romantic movement. Let us hope that he will have permanently disarmed the attitude of mind that could entitle a book *The Tyranny of Greece over Germany*. Professor Heimann's study of Saint Jerome takes us back to the borderland of paganism and Christianity, when the classics could have become museum pieces, visible and useless like the inventions in the Erewhonian Book of the Machines; instead, the vitality of the classics and the genius, however imperfect, of Jerome and the Fathers like him transmuted them and saved them for a life that still continues. It is at this stage that the concept of humanism underwent its most radical development since the fifth century B.C., and we may well wonder if we do not now stand at another parting of the ways. If we do, as Professor Babcock suggests, then we may take courage from that distant confrontation of the pagan classics and the Christian Fathers and hope that once again the classics will be a vital part of whatever new humanistic tradition emerges.

Since the contributions gathered here were delivered orally at a symposium, the limitations of time compelled us to leave out significant stages in the history of the classical tradition. Professor McDonald touches comprehensively on the great classical renaissances of the Carolingian Age and of the Italian Renaissance, but the inquiring reader will nevertheless miss a more detailed consideration of those periods. The parallels between our own time and the eighth century are obvious and misleading. According to Sir Compton Mackenzie (as quoted in the *Illustrated London News* for April 25, 1970, p. 13) "The time will come when . . . it will indeed be a distinguished person who can read"—an ominous reminder of an earlier dark age. Few now study Latin, fewer still understand it, and Greek is virtually excluded from all but the most rarified levels of academic pursuits. Yet knowledge of the Greek and Roman civilizations is more widespread than it ever has been, and the potential for spreading the classical humanities through the printed word and the media of mass communication is there to be realized. The eighth century had its Alcuin and its Charlemagne who, although (in Gibbon's phrase) "his own studies were tardy, laborious and imperfect," yet was the patron of distinguished teachers and scholars and the unwavering supporter of education and its concomitant revival of learning. The scholar-teachers of our time no less need encouragement by the leaders of their society, who in a democracy must lead in response to the wishes and tastes of the people. The problem, then, of preserving an ancient and fundamental tradition is infinitely more complex, and its solution must depend even more on devoted and widespread education by the trustees of that tradition than on patronage by the rich and powerful, whether they are governments or individuals.

The Italian Renaissance, like fifth-century Athens, is proof of the need for a commitment by society in general to humanistic ideals if those ideals are to be a part of a living educational and intellectual milieu. The patronage of the Church and the wealthy could not alone have enabled a Petrarch or a Poggio to revitalize classical learning, without a more generally favorable climate of opinion. In the limited society of the city-state, where a single man or family could sway the whole people, these favorable conditions were brought into existence with comparative ease. Yet the task is not impossible with a modern democracy living in the post-McLuhan age. If we, as classical humanists, conceive our task to be merely the conservation of the classical tradition, we shall betray our trust, and our studies will inevitably be the preserve of an elite, to many of whom the classical languages and cultures will be as much a social passport as an intellectual stimulus. This has already proved to be the case in some European countries, where the end result may yet be the elevation of the classics to the status of museum exhibits. On the other hand, if we conceive our mission to be the vitalizing of the educational and intellectual life of society, then our opportunities are limitless if our courage is great and we have imagination to match it. For "democratic" in education need not mean acceptance of the lowest common denominator, and the instruments of mass communication need not be the enemies of liberal studies but their potent allies.

It is here that Goethe's unity of the beginning and the end falls into place. The classical teacher and scholar is uniquely equipped to speak to the modern age in its own terms though his own intellectual foundations are laid in that distant past which is itself the basis of western culture. His humanism interprets the human ideal in terms that change from age to age while always drinking from the endless fountain of classical antiquity. Greek humanism was adopted by Rome; Roman humanism fused with Christianity; the Frankish barbarians gave new life to classical literature; the Italian Renaissance rediscovered the literature, thought, and art of the Greeks and Romans and used them as a living part of contemporary cultural life; the German romantics and their contemporaries were equally true to the classical ideal and, at the same time, were men of their own time. In our time the opportunities and obstacles are as great as in the times of those earlier challenges; it is the privilege, and the challenge, of the classical teacher to show to his contemporaries the unchanging values that underlie an ever changing culture. The true classicist is he who, like Blake's bard, "present, past and future sees," and with integrity unites his knowledge of the truths of the past with a sympathetic understanding of the changing present.

The Endless Fountain
Essays on Classical Humanism

by Charles L. Babcock

I

The Classics and the New Humanism

"Is the present moment the portent of a new epoch of history, a new age of humanity, a new sort of humanism, a new type of man?" [1] The question is John Courtney Murray's concerning the future of humanistic education; and from his question, I have taken the New Humanism of my title. Any person with a background in the humanities—indeed, most persons trained in what we have called the liberal arts—will recognize that I have deliberately chosen to speak of the classics in relation to a concept whose ultimate definition is likely to rest with the individual. The pluralistic nature of our educational system may justify this intentional vagueness, but, even more, the scope of any concept developed on the root *human-* demands it. I have therefore resisted the temptation to use the term *humanities* for the compelling reason that within the framework of higher education we are in a continuing crisis of definition of the humanities and their place in that framework. The educational humanities will not be far from my thinking, as you will see, but the concern will be more with their implication than with their curricular position.

An additional prefatory note will reveal where some early thoughts were leading. I first submitted as a title "The Classics as the New Humanism," and then modi-

3

fied my intent by shifting from *as* to *and* under a clutch of pressures among which can be discerned practicality, candidness, reasonable doubt, and some timidity.

We are witnessing the emergence of a New Humanism as perhaps the most vital educational force in our present experience. It is educational because it emanates in good part from those whose age places them within or just beyond our years of formal education, or from those who play some role in formal education. It is educational because it seeks to define, analyze, and make persuasive and finally effective a set of ideas and accompanying data designed to improve our performance as members of society. It is educational because in its very emergence it is teaching us something about ourselves, our institutions, and our future.

The New Humanism is no single force attributable solely to a simplistic credo, a uniform group of doctrines, an accepted body of texts, or one articulate and persuasive spokesman, although it benefits from, or is hampered by, all of these at times. It is, rather, an attitude, a concern, a questioning, a criticism, a searching, a determination. Although many of its origins are in education, it has roots in, and surely now pervades, politics, religion, business, and society—in fact, defying such compartmentalization, all parts of our lives. If any one thing unites it, it would be a central issue throughout that puts the focus on man, social and individual, as he relates to his environment, physical and social (taking this last word as inclusive of all the man-made systems that affect the individual in his living). New? Certainly not. Humanism? By any broad definition. New Humanism? If it succeeds, as it has dramatically in the past decade, in requiring two generations to pause, to take stock of themselves and their attitudes, to revise their relationships one to the other, and to affirm the humanity of their goals. Yes. New Humanism.

In 1972 I need do little to fill in the outline suggested above, for we are all affected by this force and are inescapably a part of it. Because of this involvement, however, the historical portion of Father Murray's question must be approached with caution; and the observer must recognize that he looks from within, even as a part of, a series of events. He must therefore content himself with the role of reporter, denied the advantage of perspective and the possibility of objectivity essential to the historian. John P. Roche, warning against the "instant historians" of the Kennedy-Johnson years, reminds us impressively of the limitation imposed by our very contemporariness:

> To be specific, I doubt that any historically valid treatment of the Kennedy-Johnson era can emerge for at least another decade, if then. I confess that when I emerged from the White House I signed up to do an "insider volume," but sober, professional second thoughts have led me to put that project on ice until at least 1980. The problem is that I simultaneously know too much, but not enough. I know what I thought was happening, what others on the staff thought was happening, what the press thought was happening. But I cannot fully document what happened. And I have seen enough highly classified documents to know that what most of the observers thought was happening was at best half-right.[2]

And yet, like the political strategists, those of us in education who are observers and participants in recent developments have not the choice to wait "at least another decade" to assess what is happening and then make the appropriately wise decisions. We are a part of a process that has generally prospered by a self-imposed and self-regulated slowness to change and that has prided itself on a conservative attitude because of confidence in what it was preserving. Suddenly (as time has been understood in our world), our process of change must be accelerated and probably altered. And how ill-equipped we are for either acceleration or alteration is demonstrated by the frustrations besetting the efforts of administrative and curricular bodies in all our institutions.

Because we must recognize the force of the New Humanism and use its criticisms and its suggestions in providing a current education that does not ignore the past and does prepare for the future, in some way we must again be convinced of the validity of now and of what we do now, despite our inability to assess its consequences. Perhaps Hannah Arendt has described our time in a comment that seems also to respond to Father Murray, when she notes the circular movement from thought to action and back to thought that has dominated the earlier generations of this century:

> Whereby it would be of some relevance to notice that the appeal to thought arose in the odd in-between period which sometimes inserts itself into historical time when not only the later historians but the actors and witnesses, the living themselves, become aware of an interval in time which is altogether determined by things that are no longer and by things that are not yet. In history, these intervals have shown more than once that they contain the moment of truth.[3]

Many who are critical of education today would be happy with the formulation "things that are no longer" and would be glad to grasp "things that are not yet" as an immediate goal, say, for tomorrow. But to some extent our generation of educators may best be able to play the activist role being forced upon it by accepting Miss

Arendt's "odd in-between period" as descriptive of our time. The fact that our predecessors often must have felt justified in seeking similar solace or stimulus in the face of their seemingly overwhelming obstacles should not deny us our brief moment of assumed uniqueness.

The call to us for action has been loud, often raucous, usually uncompromising, and too frequently violent. It has been dismissed as immature, illogical, irrational, impossible, and unwise, and yet for whatever reasons, and some of them may be less than admirable, we and our institutions are responding to the call for change in structure, and our academic bodies are beginning to accelerate the metamorphosis that has been their natural continuing state, no matter how the critics may assume that for their generation change has stopped or is too agonizingly slow. We are far enough into this process to see at work some of the stabilizing tensions, a polarization between those for whom no change can be fast enough and those for whom any change is at the least questionable, and the emergence, at least for a while, of a kind of progressive conservatism that may, if given the opportunity, bring about the necessary changes. Acceptance of criticism has been remarkable—indeed, I consider it the most remarkable and least appreciated part of the whole unsettling process. The need for change and the recognition that much in our system is subject to legitimate criticism have now become canonical first statements for spokesmen of nearly all parts of the spectrum. Only after these axiomatic professions do the differences in substance, method, or degree reveal a continuing state of perplexity.

Let me narrow our consideration to the process of liberal education to which our colleges of arts and sciences in American higher education have addressed themselves. Assessing the qualities of leadership in an academic speech of 1913, Viscount Haldane, then Lord Chancellor, provides a remarkable condensation of the goals of liberal education as we have understood them. Noting that "youth, with its elasticity and boundless energy, is the time to lay the foundations of wide knowledge and catholic interests," he says:

> Every man and woman is, after all, a citizen in a State. Therefore let us see to it that there is not lacking that interest in the larger life of the social whole which is the justification of a real title to have a voice and a vote. Literature, philosophy, religion, are all widening interests. So is science, so are music and the fine arts. Let every one concern himself with these or such of them as he thinks can really appeal to him. So only will his outlook be wide enough to enable him to fill his station and discharge his duties with distinction. He ought to be master of much knowledge besides that of his profession. He must try to think greatly and widely.[4]

Some of us who have tried to write catalog statements about the purpose of a liberal education and the goal of the bachelor of arts degree could have profited from Lord Haldane's presence. This is what we have professed as our goal and have hoped we were accomplishing in liberal arts training. The motto of my own university, which scarcely limits itself to the liberal arts in its offerings, says it simply: *Disciplina in civitatem.*

But apparently we have not succeeded in providing our educative goals with a structure or an attitude that insured their accomplishment by our students. So we are being told, and large numbers of us are accepting the criticism as valid. Arland F. Christ-Janer, president of the College Board, encapsules the indictment in an examination of future priorities for the board:

> The harsh reality is that people are fed up with abstractions which cannot be seen as relevant to intellectual, spiritual,

and visceral needs. Right for the role of education is the
enhancement of the future and mankind's place in it. The
future is filled with unsureness. Too often it cannot be
adequately perceived.

At the present, the educational system is thought of as
inadequate to the necessary preparation for a future which
contains the marvelous and sometimes overwhelming constant of rapid change. In reaction to criticisms we have become preoccupied with the present moment, and we are
overlooking the unavoidable insistence of the future. As a
result, the educational institutions are living with too short
and narrow a perspective as they develop their programs of
study and education. To be sure, there are those who insist
that it is only the present that matters. These voices must be
resisted, for they tend to prevent the educational institutions
from their larger mission, which is to chart the way into the
future and in some sense to live in that future.[5]

If that future is to be shaped by our current awareness
of our dilemma, as it is thus bluntly set down, what kinds
of modification can we envision? I use *modification*
pointedly, and I am well aware that it may seem to some
to be an inadequate response, for it may imply little adjustment and guarantees only some degree of change. It
is not a revolutionary word, and there are those who feel
sincerely, and express forcefully, the need for such
sweeping educational change that only *revolutionary*
aptly describes it. To justify such an apparently bland
word, I would suggest two reasons. The first is practical:
the mass is too large to tolerate quick, drastic changes
without repercussions in the development of several student generations. The second is perhaps emotional, but I
prefer to think of it as intellectual as well: the system
has worked and has such a weight of soundness in it that
I believe those student generations need not be disrupted.
My generation and those before mine have benefited
almost beyond conception from the American commit-

ment to education. And this is more than middle-aged complacency; it is frank admiration for a system that has through educational opportunity achieved for a nation of immigrants much more than the most visionary shaper of its beginnings could have imagined. Lest I sound inanely starry-eyed, I am well aware that American education has had to endure enormous strain to accomplish its charge, which Henry Steele Commager phrases thus:

> The story is familiar, how, especially in the nineteenth century, we required our schools to train citizens competent to govern themselves (a requirement not urgent in the Old World), to absorb and Americanize millions of newcomers from the Old World and elsewhere, to encourage and strengthen national unity, and to teach the habits and practices of democracy and equality and religious tolerance.[6]

If the charge now requires a different emphasis, and Commager develops the theory that our schools may be a victim in the twentieth century of their success in the nineteenth, I am not prepared to accept that the whole fabric must be scrapped and a new one substituted. Education, after all, combines a fiduciary with a hermeneutic role, and these are particularly qualities of the liberal arts. In fact, they are the primary qualities of the educational humanities. Part of the trust implied is historical and part is strikingly contemporary. A provocative reminder of this mixed trust is set down by R. J. Kaufmann:

> Humanists seem to me most authentic when they resist being exhausted by mere historicity. There is something balky about us; a brand of holy stupidity obliges us to ask questions about what has been left out of persuasive social syntheses. We are frequently off to one side giving artificial

respiration to qualities of experience which, being under-
valued in the contemporary ethos, slip into a limbo where
all those things not easily "conceived" undergo the pragmatic equivalent of historical death. . . . Bluntly, humanists
are people delegated to articulate and service an ecology of
survival values.[7]

I like the abrasiveness of these qualifying remarks on
humanists, and they seem to me to strike just the right
note of stimulation to those professing the humanities.
Much of the strength of our position will lie in the historical experience of which we are both guardians and
purveyors, but our worth is to be found in our success
in offering the values engendered by that experience to
the generations of the future. Since the classics have long
been central to humanistic learning and teaching, and
since Kaufmann's remarks could be read by some as a
justification for the sidelining of the humanities, the
classicist in particular should recognize in these remarks
the limitations they suggest and the very positive results
implicit in their conclusion.

At least four facets of this century's educational trend
provide useful perspectives to the present position of the
classics. In large part they are factors of the years following World War II, but the longer view is more pertinent. First, education has extended upward and outward to embrace incredible numbers of students and to
take a spiraling percentage of them to its upper levels.
Second, the liberal arts, which were traditionally dominant in the curricula of secondary and higher education,
survived the impact of the land-grant institutions but
have had to share the field increasingly with technical,
vocational, and professional programs. Third, the scientific explosion has provided a major impulse toward the
scientizing of all disciplines, and the humanities have

worked hard to develop scientific structure and method. Finally, and perhaps as a direct result of all the above, specialization has for some years shaped the curriculum, the preparation of the teacher, and the preoccupation of teacher and student alike at the higher levels of the system. These facets of substance, size, method, and approach have become our facts of life; they represent defensible—in part, admirable—developments. The greater proportion of students educated reflects much credit on our democratic system; we have much need for the product of the more practical educational programs; systematization of knowledge, implied in "scientizing," is a practical aid to the analysis and presentation of that knowledge; the specialist should be more equipped to command and present his material than the person less specialized. But a part of the criticism I have attributed to the New Humanism asserts that much of the resulting education now fails to meet the needs of present and future generations. Part of the complaint is that the factors of size, substance, method, and approach as shaped by these trends have effected a dehumanizing of the process, the goals, and the results. And it follows that, if education is neither humane nor human, then the system that offers it must be wrong and much be changed.

If change is thus posited as a necessity, and we seem to be accepting that it is in some degree, what of the classics? How are they to assist in that change to assure the best results for the student, the most promising route to the broader goals of humanistic education?

We have already begun to take the first mandatory step as agents for this change and in response to the curricular imperatives that have in part anticipated it. In the years since the classics relinquished their absolute hold on higher education, we have begun to find ways to offer the experience of the classics to many students for whom the approach is made only through their own language. Although the classicist had long recognized that new translations of the classics were needed for new generations of readers, and although distinguished new versions of Homer and Vergil made these classics available to the general reader as masterworks, defenders of the traditional curriculum came late to the acceptance of the classics in translation as a legitimate part of the formal educational experience. That acceptance was mainly a pragmatic one. With a few exceptions it came in the aftermath to the academic revolution that saw the elimination of requirements in the ancient languages as the foundation for an undergraduate liberal education, and the development of the broad areas of humanities, social sciences, and physical, or natural, sciences as the new structural basis for that education. The history of that modification is well documented, as is the compensatory modification in our offerings. I would only note that the modification in classical offerings continued apace during that remarkable period of numerical expansion in higher education that followed World War II, and at a time when students were electing the languages in gratifying numbers if in less gratifying percentages. As classicists, we applied the benefits of our unexpected status as a defense-oriented discipline to the professional levels of our work, and perhaps thereby set back the effectiveness of our general education, to which we clearly felt less commitment, even at times when demands on general classics courses seemed often beyond our ability to meet.

Statistics are available to show that at most levels of instruction in the classical languages, numbers are static or decreasing (such pleasant exceptions as rising elections in beginning Greek cannot counter this). At the same time, there is healthy interest in our courses that do not require the languages, courses in the literatures in translation, in civilization, in mythology, and the like. The local status of language requirements and of general distribution requirements that include a humanities segment is a significant factor in the assessment of these fluctuations, but it should not conceal the continuing recognition by succeeding generations of students that the classics provide a stimulating and productive educational experience.

An obvious concurrent shift is now suggesting itself in response to the concern about specialization. In his personal and professional commitment, the classicist is having to realize that he has been almost too successful in that trend toward specialization and systematization of his discipline, which I have called "scientizing." So successful, in fact, that he has come dangerously close to professing his subject in ways that justified the charge of dehumanization. All too often we have become specialists in a narrowing fashion, have found our best teaching experiences in the technically oriented course of restricted and usually advanced material, and have gained our rewards from the scholarly development of such specialization. The resultant imbalance, both in the individual scholar and in the presentation of the classics to students, has been recognized for some time; in distorted form it became an issue in the postwar controversy dubbed "publish or perish." In outcome, however, our constituents began to feel that we thought it more important to stress the language and its technicalities or its variations than to consider what was being said in that language and what it might mean to them. An overgeneralization, perhaps, but the fact remains that we classicists shared in this criticism to an unfortunate degree with our fellow disciplines in the liberal arts. Always excepting the personal intellectual rapport between teacher and student, we seemed to be inviting commitment to a science and not a culture, to structural analysis rather than communication, to systematics rather than an appreciation of our intellectual ancestry, and to institutions devoid of the people who created them or whom they served.

Gerald Else, one of our most able and balanced of classical spokesmen among educators and politicians, recently noted that even into our century the humanities were the classics as we think of them. The change in outlook just mentioned can be highlighted with his interpretation of the aims of the old humanities, the classics, beyond the verbal study:

> Yet language was not the be-all and end-all of the old humanities, at least in their best periods. I will assert that they had three modes or points of impact, each with its own educational purpose: first, they worked in and through *language*, aiming to develop educated taste; second, they worked with and on *the mind*, aiming to develop educated judgment and persuasiveness; and third, they operated in and upon *the whole man*, aiming to make him a moral person and a responsible citizen or political leader—in other words, a free man.[8]

Else is saying here that the classicist's role as humanistic educator is essentially the role described by Lord Haldane. Horace summed it up most neatly in his comment on the role of poets in *Ars Poetica* 333: *aut prodesse volunt aut declectare poetae.*

In his essay *De officiis* Cicero, one of the great humanists, dwelt on a philosophical distinction not new to him but characteristic of ancient and modern value systems alike: *quid utile* and *quid dulce,* what is useful and what is pleasant. So also the Roman concerned himself much with what he ought to do, *quid decet,* and what was morally (that is, by divine sanction) right or wrong, *fas* or *nefas*. Ethical systems from Socrates in Plato to Alfred North Whitehead and Paul Tillich have sought such understanding of man's social responsibility to himself and to his fellow, and have questioned social, political, or educational structures that seem to have eschewed that responsibility in their pattern of growth or success.

The best of the questions we are being asked by our students now are certainly moral questions. They stem from a vital concern for personal identity, for consciousness of self, and for self-in-society. This concern is not new. What is new, and hence the concept of New Humanism, is that young people now are transferring that self-searching to an intensive look at the system, whatever manifestation of it they may see, and asking how it aids or hinders the human values they seek in themselves and for others. In their own way they have espoused a form of Roman *humanitas*, looking for that combination of moral and intellectual excellence and that breadth of personal viewpoint fundamental to the Roman ideal. They are saying what we as classical humanists have been saying but perhaps not practicing convincingly: that technical skills are essentially mnemonic, and that thought and character are developed only through broad experience; that human relations may well be fostered by technical skills, but they can survive only if moral and intellectual excellence and commitment show the way. Young people question that such a goal can be achieved in education through the course distribution or general requirements and ask for a near-total permissiveness in the curricular package as their prescription for its achievement. In the end they resent the normative tenor of the older generation and criticize the essentially descriptive limitations we have placed on the process of education. Despite the rhetoric of the individual that has recently been dominant, there is clearly a moral thrust in the New Humanism that should respond to a liberal education, if that education can reassert the values that shaped it to the present generation. The militant critics have forced these considerations; but we have noted widespread support and acceptance of their criticisms and concern for a reassessment of priorities, of moral values, of courses of public action and private activity, and, ultimately, for a redefinition of individual and corporate responsibilities and goals. The whole educational system stands accused, but if the humanistic attitudes of present students shape the accusation, then those disciplines most surely endowed with humanistic potential and tradition must look to themselves and face what O. Meredith Wilson has written of as "The Dilemma of Humanistic Education": "Humanistic education has been engrossed with the problem of how best to sharpen the intellect. By what means do we help our child to fulfill his 'human potential'?" [9]

Let me juxtapose two ideas mentioned earlier, the fiduciary and hermeneutic qualities of education—and, in particular, of humanistic education—when brought to bear on what Professor Kaufmann called the humanist's delegated task, articulation of an ecology of survival values. Appreciation of this confluence should remind the classicist of the quality of his subject, its incredible breadth, its proven value-oriented potential, and its claim on the meaning of the adjective that describes it, *classicus*. I need not rehearse the canon of what we have to offer in the way of idea, literary form, cultural and social institution, humanity and inhumanity, logic and faith. The list is long, exciting, varying, and universally useful. Yes, Cicero's *utile* happily combines with his *dulce*, as does Horace's *prodesse* with his *delectare*, if we remember that we are dealing with the values of our heritage. Those values cannot be allowed the luxury of somnolence or burial even in an era when we are bombarded daily with such an overwhelming number of new facts and interpretations that yesterday and tomorrow have to fight for attention. If we as classical humanists are trustees and interpreters of the past, then we must not let the present's seeming unwillingness or inability to hear obscure the universal values that we are transmitting. These works "of the first class" have not only created our ideas and our vocabulary for their use, but they have taught us how to develop, warp, or reject them. Their values are those by which we live, or, if you will, those against which we rebel. The manner by which our instruction imparts this concept will vary. Because of the vitality of the cultures of antiquity and the unceasing pertinence of what they have given us, there is a natural danger in the process of interpretation, as noted by David Porter:

> I have much sympathy for the demand of our students that their education be relevant to their lives, but the problem is far more complex than they sometimes realize. Nothing is easier, to take an obvious example, than to make the *Trojan Women* relevant to American involvement in Vietnam, and few classes do not respond to such a treatment. The difficulty is that by making this connection, provocative in itself, we may suggest to our students that this alone is significant about the play, whereas the fact is that the *Trojan Women* is still with us precisely because its significance transcends any one time or place, be it 415 B.C. or 1970 A.D. Thus, the real danger is that by stressing the particular relevance of the Classics to our time we may unintentionally obscure the even more important fact of their general relevance to all times and places.[10]

The relevant is so often not recognized at the time, perhaps in part because its importance is essentially individual and only by educated transferal is it applicable to broader social concerns. The humanist must constantly rethink his teaching with this in mind, return constantly to the great issues and suppress all but the necessary deviations therefrom that may form the current excitement of his research and therefore should breathe life into his teaching. The scientized humanities can become the trivialized humanities. But we must also remember that relevance, real value, cannot in the flowering of man's mind be confined to those areas that allow immediate and practical application. Relevance, if it is to strengthen the culture that can improve itself, must allow for the detailed and seemingly narrow examination of man's accomplishments and mistakes, putting the puzzle of man's human strengths and weaknesses together. Then can the humanist contribute to the self-understanding students seek, and then can he satisfy both the urge to know and to understand, in which ethical choice is always at question, and the responsibility to serve, whether in the transmission of knowledge and the interpretation of principles or in the extension of a helping hand to a staggering individual or society.

Loren Eiseley, a marvelously sensitive interpreter of the human experience and an able anthropologist, has some sensible words about the misconception of academic relevance. He is speaking of one of his professors, whose own awakening to the field of anthropology he has just described:

> I absorbed much from him, though I hasten to make the reluctant confession that he was considerably beyond thirty. Most of what I learned was gathered over cups of coffee in a dingy campus restaurant. What we talked about were things some centuries older than either of us. Our common interest lay in snakes, in scapulimancy, and other forgotten rites of benighted forest hunters.

I have always regarded this man as an extraordinary individual, in fact, a hidden teacher. But alas, it is all now so old-fashioned. We never protested the impracticality of his quaint subjects. He was an excellent canoeman, but he took me to places where I fully expected to drown before securing my degree. To this day, fragments of his unused wisdom remain stuffed in some back attic of my mind. Much of it I have never found an opportunity to employ, yet it has somehow colored my whole adult existence.[11]

Loren Eiseley is one whose career and talents might well guide us in relating the classics to the world of education in which we now live and the direction of which we hope to influence. Eiseley fits, as well as any person I have known, the definition of a modern Renaissance man, one who has broad interests and has been able to develop his knowledge in a number of areas well beyond the superficial. He is a scientist and a humanist, and he has found a medium for expression of each capacity that denies the individuality of neither and demonstrates that there is no mutual exclusion in either. His literary competence is of the highest order, his scientific accomplishment matches it, and his books combine the two admirably. His whole career has been academic, and yet he has managed to talk of the ordinary experience of growing up and wondering about nature and people in terms that combine philosophical and anthropological depth with poetic beauty.

I dwell on Eiseley for two reasons. First, he demonstrates in his own personal achievement and in his intellectual qualities what I believe we should have in our educational thinking: the retreat from the exclusiveness of specialization into the more productive climate wherein the specialist recognizes his responsibility to the general needs of society and works toward the reuniting of the disciplines to that end. Second, if we in the classics are to profess our field fairly in such a climate, we must alter our training patterns in such ways as to produce a modern Renaissance man of Eiseley's type as the classicist for the future. These two assessments are not necessarily to be separated. They seem to me to be extensions of what the academic classicist has been doing in the past, from which he has allowed the climate and the pressures of mid-twentieth-century education to distract him.

Lord Snow's celebrated "two cultures" have in recent years been subjected to much scrutiny. Few question that one "does" science and the arts in different ways, but there is much question about the artificiality of the self-imposed separation between the scientist and the artist or the humanist. Werner Heisenberg has recently attempted to demonstrate the humanistic milieu in which he and such scientists as Bohr, Planck, Fermi, and Einstein evolved the physics that has so deeply affected our lives.[12] In another area, the chemist Roger Williams pleads for a closer relationship between biology and behavioral science by arguing from a biological standpoint that "the recognition of the uniqueness of human minds is essential to human understanding." [13] And yet only a short time ago, as I prefer to view it, when in 1941, I was a freshman at Berkeley, there was still amusement that psychology had been legitimized by being inscribed in monumental letters on a building completed less than a decade earlier to house the life sciences. How many of us remember psychology as a life science within our educational experience?

The New Humanism, I believe, has challenged us to remember that education has become overcompartmentalized, that these separations, though potentially valuable for the isolation of fact and the securing of technological advance, run the risk of failing the student and the society that he represents by neglecting the reintegration of knowledge thus achieved for the individual and social good. Cannot science and the humanities reunite in education to achieve again something of the common sense that would not separate them in antiquity? Surely the reason for the remarkable preference shown for the social and behavioral sciences by students these days is not the joy they find in quantified data but their belief that these areas of study are humane in the best sense of the word and that they have the ultimate interest of individual and social man as their purpose. Have we in the humanities not lost our purpose if that degree of humaneness is not pellucid in our teaching?

If we are too compartmentalized, is interdisciplinary activity a remedy? In part it surely is, and the classics have long been interdisciplinary in their offerings. The classicist who is not at least a cultivated amateur in history, archaeology, art, and philosophy is not whole. Although literature has been central to our discipline, we, as interpreters of civilizations and cultures, have been led into a variety of neighboring disciplines and have been required to speak with at least modest expertise as we look at, say, economic or technological aspects of the ancient world. But perhaps we have been too hesitant in advancing beyond the frontiers of the humanities as we have looked for interdisciplinary relationships to which our insights might contribute. The University of Michigan's Center for Ancient and Modern Studies has certainly shown the way in expanding the interfacing of the classical humanities with the social and behavioral sciences. Studies of ancient science and technology are becoming more frequent, and they are not limited to the admirable aegis of the historian of science; many are written by classicists drawn to them from literary problems. The political scientist is surely as natural a colleague for the interdisciplinary classicist as is the philosopher or the specialist in another literature. The excited response of the engineer or the premedical student or the physicist or the sociologist to the newly discovered world of antiquity in a course in Greek or Roman civilization has offered us the challenge. As strict constructionists, we have been cautious in reminding ourselves that "interdisciplinary" suggests and even demands solid disciplines among which the relationships can be explored, and rightly so. But experience has bred increasing confidence in our ability to define the curricular content of such courses and to recognize that the gray areas of overlap are not devoid of color content. Interdisciplinary explorations will continue to play an increasing part in our impact on liberal education.

"Education," says Charles Silberman, "is becoming the gateway to the middle and upper reaches of society, which means that the schools and colleges thereby become the gatekeepers of society." [14] This remark is made in a context that points to the inevitable politicizing of educational institutions in this role, but it should remind us as well of our responsibility as the shapers of the consciousness of that society. The student trying to define for himself whence his New Humanism derives and where it should lead has instinctively expected the humanities—D. L. Stevenson's "culturally defining arts" [15]— to show him how to approach the problems that he and his society face. The humanist as "ecologist of survival values" has his task set for him, and it must not be interpreted to mean that the survival is his alone.

You will remember that we once believed in committing to memory great passages of literature or noble sayings from the past as guides to our own emerging values or as items of pleasure or comfort for moments when either was needed. Literature, the classics, whether the works of the first order from antiquity or from later cultures, provided to the educated or even to the partially educated person rich entertainment for his spirit, stimulation for his mind, precepts for his choice of action, and examples for his daily life; the classics shared with religion the larger part of his intellectual and spiritual activity. Cicero caught the importance of literature in a world we still struggle to understand in a few lines of his speech for Archias. Those over forty will have learned them and have been moved by them:

> Nam ceterae neque temporum sunt neque aetatum omnium neque locorum; at haec studia adulescentiam acuunt, senectutem oblectant, secundas res ornant, adversis perfugium ac solacium praebent, delectant domi, non impediunt foris, pernoctant nobiscum, peregrinantur, rusticantur. (*Arch.* 16)

We are being advised here, of course, of the value of the *studia litterarum* both for the formation of character and the pleasure of the mind, of which they are, Cicero assumes, *remissio humanissima ac liberalissima*—words of a Roman consular in a dubious defense of a Greek poet in a world that can mean little to the now generation.

But the classical humanist knows that Cicero's words are words that are normative to the culture of the West and have established what we have been, what we might have been, who we are, and who we might be. It matters little that few of us are directly descended from that Roman culture or from the Greek that informed it. The fabric of what we are as a multiracial, many- or single-classed, pluralistic society has been prepared—sometimes misguidedly, more often with inspiration—from the continuing reinterpretation and expression of the ideas that were shaped in the millennium centered on the birth of Jesus and of the Roman empire. Much of antiquity has only historical value for the present, though much of it is as pertinent to us now and for the future as ever before. Thus the questions asked, the perceptions offered, the pleasures and horrors chronicled, the searching for self and society in a rapidly expanding world, move far beyond the historical and the limits of the practical as they speak to the individual who seeks them out.

May I illustrate by two short quotations from a statement by Christine Philpot Clark, a black student of the classics as an undergraduate at Bryn Mawr and now a lawyer in New York City with an impressive record in civil rights and civic concerns:

> I fought back thoughts about how irrelevant to my later life my studies were, noting such thoughts were common to *everyone* seeking a liberal arts education. I now think that had I pursued the *racial* roots for my particular uneasiness about the relevance of my studies, I would have felt absurd and would probably have never finished college, Bryn Mawr or anywhere else. But the College helped me through the crisis. And I'll never forget it. As a result I work free for only two efforts: black liberation and Bryn Mawr College.

Mrs. Clark concludes her remarks with a comment of shattering pertinence:

> Bryn Mawr did give me much of my capacity to cope, joy in discipline, and strength in gaining knowledge. The College led me to past worlds and hopes about future ones. It taught me to spot weak motivation (including my own), to question fallacious reasoning and to devise rational alternatives. These gifts are not only nice words; they are useful in destroying racism.[16]

The New Humanism is an uncompromising force. Its proponents have the same task their elders had, self-knowledge and understanding of the environment in which that self must function. But they are angry with what they are learning of themselves and of how the environment, physical and social, falls short of the human and technological potential that they have seen surrounding them as they have grown to adulthood. They are totally committed to rectifying the shortcomings, human and technological. Their commitment should be catching, as Henry Hewes suggests in his review of the play *The Trial of the Catonsville Nine:*

> To attend this play is to go to the Good Shepherd-Faith Church on West 66th Street and make a token atonement for the incompleteness of our commitment. We do not even have to be in political agreement with these radicals. We only need to feel that whatever it is we believe, we believe it too half-heartedly.[17]

We cannot believe half-heartedly in the value of the classics as a continuing source of individual and social advantage in education, both formal and informal. They have something to say of value to the New Humanist, whose newness consists of his commitment with its sense of human urgency. To it we can respond with the flexibility allowed by quality and the conviction that real values transcend importunities even for those importuning. If we redirect our own commitment, it will speak to that of others.

Nil desperandum, Horace has Teucer advise his companions (*Odes* I.7.27 and 30–32):

> o fortes peioraque passi
> mecum saepe viri, nunc vino pellite curas;
> cras iterabimus aequor.[18]

1. "On the Future of Humanistic Education," in *Humanistic Education and Western Civilization: Essays for Robert M. Hutchins,* ed. Arthur A. Cohen (New York, 1964), p. 231.

2. "The Jigsaw Puzzle of History," *New York Times Magazine,* 24 January 1971, p. 15.

3. *Between Past and Future: Six Exercises in Political Thought* (New York, 1961), p. 9.

4. *The Conduct of Life and Other Addresses* (New York, 1915), p. 22.

5. "The College Board at 70: Priorities for the Future," *College Board Review* 78 (Winter 1970–71): 14–15, College Entrance Examination Board, New York. Reprinted by permission.

6. *The Commonwealth of Learning* (New York, 1968), p. 5.

7. "On Knowing One's Place: A Humanistic Meditation," *Daedalus,* Summer 1969, pp. 708–9.

8. "The Old and the New Humanities," *Daedalus,* Summer 1969, pp. 803–4.

9. "The Dilemma of Humanistic Education," in *Humanistic Education and Western Civilization,* p. 101.

10. "Classics in Translation: Some Comments and Some Suggestions," *The Classical World* 63 (1970): 290–91. Reprinted by permission.

11. *The Unexpected Universe* (New York, 1969), p. 63.

12. *Physics and Beyond: Encounters and Conversations,* trans. by A. J. Pomerans (New York, 1970).

13. "The Biology of Behavior," *Saturday Review* 54, no. 5 (January 30, 1971): 18.

14. *Crisis in the Classroom. The Remaking of American Education* (New York, 1970), p. 69.

15. "For the Liberal Arts College and for the Humanities," *Hunter Alumni Quarterly,* Autumn 1969, p. 13.

16. "As It Was and As It Is," *Bryn Mawr Alumnae Bulletin,* Spring 1969, pp. 5–6. Reprinted by permission.

17. "The Theatre," *Saturday Review* 54, No. 5 (March 6, 1971): 21.

18. Cf. the enthusiastic and positive use of *nil desperandum* by Jan B. Fischer, "The Classics in Revolt—*nil desperandum,*" *Classical World* 64, no. 6 (February 1971): 194–96.

by William F. McDonald

Classicism, Christianity, and Humanism

In this paper, I shall examine critically the origins, growth, and decline of the classical curriculum; the way of life that it has fostered; and the values that may be salvaged from it before it passes away. That the classics are *in extremis* has long been known. Almost fifty years ago, in 1922, George H. Stevenson, Fellow and Tutor of University College, Oxford, wrote an essay entitled, "Some Reflections on the Teaching of Roman History" in which he said: "Now we are taking in each other's washing. Schools provide universities with graduates— universities provide schoolmasters to schools." More recently, in the spring of 1958, the Association of Teachers in Technical Institutions (in Great Britain) declared war against "a limited culture dominated by the glory of Greece and the grandeur of Rome reflecting little of the achievement, the ideas and the philosophy of modern science."

A culture and a discipline that have endured for some four hundred years and during that time, for better or worse, have formed the mind and character of western Europe should not be interred without decent funeral rites. Unfortunately, I am unable to do this without being personal and autobiographical, and for this I ask your indulgence. In his inaugural address upon his induction as Professor of Medieval and Renaissance English Liter-

28

ature at the University of Cambridge in 1954, C. S. Lewis observed that the title of the new chair was significant. By joining the Middle Ages with the Renaissance, it implied that the traditional antithesis between the two had been exaggerated. I am essaying an even more radical judgment: that my education as a growing boy and the way of life that it inculcated were much closer in subject matter and temper to the schooling of the sixteenth century than is the contemporary system to that of World War I America; that there was less change in the character of western Christendom between 1600 and 1914 than there has been between 1914 and 1971.

This remarkable cultural continuity was due to a historical coincidence. In the Renaissance and for some three centuries following it, the classical spirit of Greco-Roman antiquity was joined with the Christian spirit of the Middle Ages to create Christian humanism. This was a mixed marriage and has always shown the stresses and strains of an imperfect union. Nonetheless, it bore bounteous fruit because what each had in common with the other was so precious and so intimate that the traits whereby they differed could not keep them apart. This is not to say that the betrothal was necessary. Like all betrothals it was fortuitous. None will maintain that one need be a classicist to be a Christian or a Christian to be a classicist. In the fourth century the emperor Julian attempted to impede the *sponsalia;* and in the eleventh century Saint Peter Damian tried to obtain a decree of nullity. Both failed, and in the sixteenth century the union was consummated.

There were three reasons for this: (1) in the sixteenth century the superintendence of education was almost a complete monopoly of the Christian cleric, and therefore, whatever changes might occur in the curriculum, the intent of the teachers could not be other than to confirm a Christian pupil in the Christian faith; (2) the vehicle of communication, written and oral, was the same for both Christian and classical studies—the Latin language; (3) it was shortly discovered, though through a glass darkly, that there was a subtle and salutary connection between the humanity of Jesus and the humanism of the Greco-Roman spirit. Had not Plato and Plotinus in the late classical period and Aristotle in the high Middle Ages given intellectual form to Christian philosophy and theology? Had not Vergil been baptised by Dante?

Finally, it was in the guise (or disguise, if you will) of Christianity that the fundamental Judaic concepts of the unicity of God and the complete dependence of mankind upon Him were brought to the Western world. Cardinal Manning once remarked that spiritually we are all Semites. Certainly, there is much to the contention that Christianity is Judaism made acceptable to the Gentiles. *Teste David cum Sibylla,* as the medieval hymn put it. David *and* the Sibyl were both prophetic of the new order. Thus the classical concept of the wholeness and self-sufficiency of man was joined with the Judaic concept of the absolute sovereignty of God. These two points of view seem, and indeed are, contrary, if not contradictory; and the only belief that made such a synthesis possible was the Christian doctrine of the Incarnation—*verbum caro factum,* the Word made flesh, the humanization of divinity. I remember as a young man attending church in Switzerland and hearing a sermon *De Deo ludente*—God at play. *O sancta simplicitas!* As Thomas Hardy says in his poem "Christmas Eve": "So fair a fancy few would weave in these days."

This Christian classicism, engendered in the Renaissance, became and remained the basis of the education of the youth of western Christendom from the sixteenth to the earlier part of the present century. In our times and in our country it has expressed itself most fully in the curriculum and discipline of the small American church-related liberal arts college. In the second half of the sixteenth century this type of education was no less a reality at Eton and Winchester in Anglican England than it was at Strassburg under Johann Sturm, the headmaster of the Lutheran gymnasium there; or under Calvin at Geneva; or, finally, at Messina in Sicily, where the Jesuits had opened their first school in 1542. Indeed, it may be said that if there was, at the time of the Reformation, one issue on which both middle-class and conservative Protestantism and aristocratic Catholicism agreed, it was the necessity of instituting and maintaining a Christian classical curriculum.

Myself, I received my early education at a Jesuit preparatory school and a Jesuit college. Subsequently, I was matriculated at Oxford where, in the School of Litterae Humaniores, I continued on a higher level and with little deviation from the norm my earlier education. Since then, whatever training I have received has been professional, not liberal. If the earlier years are the period in which a young man's mind and character are formed, I confess (and I say it with gratitude and affection) that I am the product of Jesuit schooling. Now, of the many manuals and treatises of instruction and guidance composed and published during the Renaissance in order to initiate this new system, the Jesuit *Ratio Studiorum*, definitively expressed in the edition of 1599, was one. There were editions before 1599 and several since then, and, taken together, they represent the most detailed and most comprehensive description of the Christian classical curriculum and its purpose. In Catholic Counterreformation Europe, the Society of Jesus enjoyed an almost complete monopoly of the education of boys; and in

Protestant Europe, however much they might differ theologically from the Catholic church and among themselves, the Church of England, the Lutheran church, and the Reformed church all agreed that the learned Christian gentleman was the Christian educated in the classical tradition. Since I have not only read but also to a degree studied the *Ratio* and (what may be more important) experienced its application and effects in my formative years, I believe that I am competent to pass judgment on it and, in doing so, on the several cognate Protestant systems directed toward the same end. I doubt that there is any school in Christendom, even a Jesuit school, where I could receive the same kind of education today. I am a relic. There are not many like us left, and you will not see our kind again.

The *Ratio* was not the invention of the Jesuit educator. Ignatius of Loyola himself declared that the model of his system was the classical curriculum already in use at the University of Paris, his own alma mater and that of his first companions. In fact, he was wont to compare the discipline of Paris with the lack of discipline in the contemporary Italian universities, and he deliberately staffed his own Roman college with Paris graduates. But the *Ratio*'s antecedents go even further back. In 1538 Johann Sturm, already identified as the Lutheran headmaster at Strassburg, published his treatise *De litterarum ludis recte aperiendis*. Indeed, Sturm and his companions contended that the Jesuits had stolen their plan from him, and none can deny that the palm of priority belongs to Pastor Sturm. The fact is, of course, that the classical contagion was already abroad, and both Ignatius and Sturm had been infected by the schools of the Brethren of the Common Life. Sturm had studied for three years (1521–24) at their college at Liège and, according to his biographers, adopted its organization as the model for his Strassburg school. Ignatius, in turn, when he began his studies at Paris, had lived at the Collège Montaigu, where the system of the Brethren already prevailed.

Before describing this curriculum, let us examine its antecedents, and first, on the classical side. There are three names associated with its development—Isocrates, Marcus Tullius Cicero, and Quintilian; and there are two works essential for its understanding—the three books of Cicero's *De Oratore* and the twelve books of Quintilian's *Institutio Oratoria*.

Let us start with Isocrates. Greek formal higher education began with the Sophists, of whom the first was Gorgias and the last and best was Isocrates. In form the word *sophistes* means a man who makes a profession of wisdom—one who makes his living by teaching for pay. Before Pericles the aristocratic code of Pindar prevailed —that male excellence (*arete*) was a combination of good breeding and beautiful bodily form, active and at rest. But Pindar was the last of the Greek aristocrats, and before he died in 438 B.C., he was disturbed by the growing insolence of Athenian imperialism and the rise in Athens of an urban proletariat of the type that later Cicero calls in Rome the *turba forensis*. After Pericles' death in 429 B.C. Cleon established the prototype of the *novus homo*, which leads to Aristotle's definition of man as a *zoon politikon*, the man who is domiciled in the polis and engages in political activity. But effectively to do this in fourth-century Athens was to study rhetoric and to excel in the art of public speaking. In an age in which there was no radio, television, or newspaper, in which reading matter was scarce and generally inaccessible, when, as Demosthenes tells us, men came in from the suburbs at dawn to ask, "What's the news?", the only way to public notice and public office was by the art of literary composition and the practice of public declamation. This was a present need for a practical end, and the sophists supplied it. For Isocrates the proper study of man was rhetoric, and his highest good was active participation in public affairs. Unlike Plato and Aristotle, Isocrates considered philosophy as propaedeutic to rhetoric, and unlike the Pre-Socratics, he viewed astronomy and geometry simply as "gymnastics of the mind." To use a later Latin phrase, to Isocrates the well-rounded man was the *bonus vir dicendi peritus*—the man who was both good *and* a good speaker.

Thus Isocrates established two principles of formal education that became in time, and thereafter remained, the foundation of a liberal discipline: (1) that the art of correct and elegant composition is fundamental in every school system; and (2) that the formation of character, moral training, which is the adaptation of the child to the mores of the community, is and should be the aim of every educational system. As to the art of composition, we must remember that to the Greek *logos* meant not only the spoken and written word but also the thought that lies behind the outward form. There is nothing that compels us to define and refine our ideas more than the requirement that we put them down in writing for everyone to see. This training in literary form, this acquisition of the three fundamental qualities of good writing, clarity, economy, and grace, became then and remained thereafter the basic discipline of the Latin grammar school.

As for the second of Isocrates' two principles, that a good orator must also be a good man, we must remember that the Greek male was not a domestic animal. He lived in the open air and not at home. His was the public assembly that voted on the propositions of the public orators. Thus the orator must be the politician and the statesman, versed in domestic and foreign policy and genuinely dedicated to the welfare of his state and fellow citizens. In this way the art of composition is raised above the level of verbal dexterity, and the public orator is put in a higher echelon than the demagogue. He deals with issues that are great and honorable, that contribute to the general welfare and happiness of mankind, and that tend to liberate the mind from mean and selfish motives and to produce that quality which Cicero, in the *De Officiis*, calls *magnanimitas*. If he does not become in Plato's words "the spectator of all time and existence," at least his vision extends beyond the frontier of his native land and his concept of human needs beyond his personal wants.

Isocrates' own life and work are an example of this broader concept of the function of rhetoric. Although he composed many speeches for others and taught rhetoric for some forty years, because of a speech deficiency he never appeared in court. He was really a tractarian, and his compositions were in effect tracts for the times. Living when the Persian menace once again appeared great and the Greek states were destroying themselves in fratricidal strife, he sought the political unity of Greece under a leading state or statesman. Appealing in turn to Athens, Sparta, and Dionysius of Syracuse, he finally found his champion in Philip of Macedon and died happily on the morrow of the battle of Chaeronea. To Isocrates, as he says in his *Panegyricus*, the word *Hellenes* should apply to those who share a common culture rather than to those who derive from a common ancestry. More than any other individual of his time, except perhaps Alexander the Great, he foresaw the Hellenistic world, and it was he who handed on the torch to Marcus Tullius Cicero.

Because Cicero was a Roman and wrote and spoke

Latin, we are apt to forget that he lived in a world society that was culturally Greek. As the Greek classical age was the period of creative literary activity, so the Greek world after Alexander was the age of conscious literary criticism and formal scholarship. Alexandria, as a contemporary writer put it, became "the hen-coop of the Muses," where grammarians, philologers, textual critics and textual commentators flourished. The literary art became a self-regarding activity in which poets wrote for other poets and coteries of scholars clustered together like bees in hives to fan one another. It was in this atmosphere and by these groups that the classical Greek authors of the golden age of Greek literature were made the paradigms of the higher education and Attic Greek, and only Attic Greek, the language of the learned class. The Latin language, on the other hand, though it was achieving literary maturity in the usage of Cicero and his contemporaries, had not yet attained that academic status which admitted it to a place in the curriculum of higher studies. Its position was not unlike the position of the vernacular languages (English, French, Spanish, and so forth) in relation to Latin in the time of the Renaissance. Accordingly, in Rome during Cicero's time all the tutors of well-born Roman boys were Greeks; and most Romans, if they could afford it, went to Greece for their graduate studies. Molon, the Rhodian ambassador, was one of Cicero's tutors, and on one occasion addressed the Roman Senate in Greek without the aid of an interpreter. Cicero spoke both literally and tropically when he remarked, "We Romans have gone to school in Greece." Note finally that by this time Greek professors of rhetoric were teaching Romans the art of composition and public oratory for the very good reason that it was in Rome now, and not in Greece, that public oratory was the path to public honor.

Cicero carried on the tradition of Isocrates in one respect and differed from it in two other respects. In the Rome of Cicero, as in the Athens of Isocrates, the teaching of rhetoric and public speaking was for use and not for pleasure. Public policy there, as in Athens earlier, was being decided by the *plebs urbana,* or, as Cicero less graciously expressed it, the *faex Romuli;* and it was only in the Forum, in the Senate, and in the lawcourts that a political program could be made public and brought to completion. But it was wherein he differed from Isocrates that Cicero made his greater contributions. To Cicero, no doubt partly as a result of his political misfortunes, the study of rhetoric for use was ancillary to the study of literature for its own sake. In moving from Rome to Tusculum, from his town house to his country villa, as the winds of political favor rose and fell, Cicero combined in a remarkable fashion the active with the contemplative life, the "slings and arrows" of the hustings with the *otium et quies* of exurbia. In the second place, unlike Isocrates, Cicero made rhetoric ancillary to philosophy. To him, as to Plato and Aristotle, the intellect was superior to the will, and the contemplative to the active life.

It is in the light of these two differences from the Isocratic formula, the cultivation of literature for its own sake and the primacy of philosophy over rhetoric, that Cicero's *De Oratore* is to be read. In the three books of this work Cicero expresses professionally his whole theory of education. This essay was published in 55 B.C., when Cicero was at the height of his fame and intellectual powers. There is nothing narrow about it. From the title one might think it is a handbook on rhetoric and oratory, or at best a technical treatise on education. It is all that, but more. It elaborates Cicero's mature views on rhetoric, literature, philosophy, history, and politics, so far as each contributes to the formation of the ideal man of the golden age of the Greco-Roman world. In it Cicero is the first to name the seven liberal arts that later were to form the *trivium* and *quadrivium* of the Middle Ages: literature, rhetoric, philosophy, mathematics, music, geometry, and astronomy. He is also the first to embrace these studies under the captions *artes liberales* and *liberalis disciplina*. In doing so, he translated into Latin and through Latin into the European languages the Greek expression *enkuklios paideia*—all-around education. The meaning of the Greek phrase is more precisely expressed in the Latin. *Liberalis* comes from *liber* and connotes freedom; not just freedom from slavery but emancipation from manual and mercenary pursuits; and the enjoyment of that *otium cum dignitate* without which what Aristotle calls "the activity of leisure" cannot be exercised. As the old Egyptian proverb put it: "A blacksmith never goes on an embassy."

Cicero's ideal is the *doctus orator:* as Crassus says, "When I am asked what is the highest excellence of all, I give the palm to the *doctus orator.*" It is he who possesses par excellence the quality of *humanitas*, and it is in the *De Oratore* that the word *humanitas* most frequently occurs. In fact, the word is almost the exclusive property of Cicero. It is interesting, in passing, to note that the Greeks thought of education as beginning with the boy (*paideia* from *pais*), and the Romans conceived it as reaching its perfection in the man (*humanitas* from *homo*). Cicero makes it clear that this ideal is not easy to attain because it involves the simultaneous achievement of two aims: the practical one of Isocrates—to make a man good and a competent public orator; and the more academic aim of Cicero—the cultivation of the more humane letters and philosophy for their own sakes. Most men will not have the nature, the ability, the opportunity, the leisure, and above all the financial means to attain them. But the Ciceronian concept of the double aim persisted, in theory if not always in fact (*Omne tulit punctum qui miscuit utile dulci*, as Horace says) until, more than a century later, the rhetorician Quintilian institutionalized and made professional the amateur program of Cicero.

Between Cicero and Quintilian the nature of Roman society changed, as Tacitus makes clear in a famous passage in his *Annals*. The old narrowly Roman *nobilitas*, which had ruled the later Republic until the revolution, was giving place to a new bureaucratic establishment made up of competent men from the more obscure Roman families, from Italy outside Rome, and from the provinces. Crassus had already observed in the *De Oratore* that the Latins were more interested in studying literature than the Romans; and later, Pliny the Younger, in a letter of recommendation on behalf of a young man, wrote, "He is fond of study like most poor men." These were the *novi homines* of the early Empire who "by good luck or by hard work," as Tacitus puts it, having achieved Roman citizenship ascended the ladder of honor (the *cursus honorum*) in the imperial civil service and attained an honorable place in the new regime. Of these the supreme example was the emperor Vespasian, a Sabine who never quite lost his rustic speech. His grandfather had been a centurion in Pompey's army; his father a tax farmer in Asia Minor; and his mother's brother the only member of his family before him to achieve the senatorial dignity. Vespasian himself started his public career as a *tribunus militum* and rose through successive stages, quaestor in Crete or Cyrene, aedile and praetor in Rome, until he became proconsul of the province of Africa. Obviously, for these men, who lived throughout the empire, the old *tirocinium fori* (the novitiate of the forum), as Quintilian calls it, was largely unavailable. Cicero, you will recall, was taken by his father to Rome and apprenticed, as it were, to the distinguished family of the Scaevolae. But this had been in the good old days, and Quintilian, although he recommended it in principle, was quite aware that it was no longer feasible in practice. Consequently, it was for the education of this new class that Quintilian wrote his *Institutio Oratoria*, the most important treatise on education in the history of western Europe in its influence upon educational practice.

Quintilian lived and taught rhetoric in the first century of our era. He was of Spanish origins and therefore by birth representative of the new order. The two generations of his life-span were not a period in which political oratory was encouraged or practiced with safety. There were of course the lawcourts, where oratorical ability was still of use; but the practice of law was now becoming professional, and law schools were springing up not only in Rome but also in the provinces, especially at Beirut. Clearly this was not the way by which the *liberalis disciplina* of Cicero was to be preserved. On the other hand, there was the need created by the growth of the new non-Roman public servants and men of letters, whose spoken tongue was either not Latin or a provincial patois of Latin. Naturally these men, moving into Roman official and literary circles, coveted the badge of civility that only a correct and urbane Latin speech and style could confer. Because the only available system whereby this urbanity could be acquired was that of the schools of rhetoric, at Rome and abroad, naturally it was to them that men of the new classes flocked. In the beginning there was chaos and a tendency toward exaggeration and artificiality in expression that is characteristic of the literary nouveau riche. *Declamatio* ran riot, and the younger Seneca justly observed, "We are being educated for the classroom and not for life." On the other hand, this was the educational background of the great writers of the silver age of Latin literature, men like the younger Seneca, Lucan, the younger Pliny, Tacitus, and, above all, Quintilian himself; and therefore it had in it the promise of the future. Vespasian, when he appointed Quintilian the first salaried professor of rhetoric in Rome, took the initial step toward its official support; and Quintilian, when he published his *Institutes* about 95 A.D., inaugurated and institutionalized a discipline that lasted almost until the fall of the western empire. The discovery by Poggio, in 1410, of the complete manuscript of this work in the monastery of Saint Gall was without doubt the most important find in the history of Renaissance and modern liberal studies. Quintilian's *Institutes* formed the model of instruction in the schools of the Low Countries conducted by the Brethren of the Common Life, where Erasmus studied, and also later at the University of Paris, where the founder of the Jesuits went to school. A contemporary of Saint Ignatius speaks of "noster Quintilianus"; and another early Jesuit, in a commentary on the *Ratio* published in 1703, cites the Spanish-born rhetorician continuously and almost exclusively as his authority.

Quintilian, although he defined the orator after the elder Cato as the *bonus vir dicendi peritus*, lived in an age when the professional practice of oratory, except in the lawcourts, was no longer the path to political preferment. Therefore, his aim was rather the *bonus vir scribendi peritus*, and his purpose the training in the Latin language and Latin literature of the well-to-do youth throughout the Empire. Consequently, a broadening of the curriculum was necessary. The latter part of Book I, which discusses grammar and language, is directly of use to every student of Latin, even today, and indirectly to every student of language. In Book X, he discusses and recommends the acquisition of good reading habits, not narrowly for rhetorical uses but broadly for the study of all literature. His analysis in the same book of the works and styles of Greek and Roman writers is a *locus classicus* in the history of literary criticism. Although Greek was read and the Greek classics taught, the emphasis was now on Latin, spoken and written, for by this time, because of the achievements of the writers of the golden age, the Latin language had replaced Greek as the language of instruction in the higher learning and was now considered in and of itself worthy of imitation. Quintilian's own Latin style is redolent of Cicero, and it is Ciceronian Latin that he makes the model of instruction in Latin prose composition—*Ex uno fere Cicerone*, as the *Ratio* later puts it. His achievement was the guarantee in the later empire of a ruling bureaucracy that was not only literate but also to a degree literary. The architects of Renaissance education built their edifice upon two foundations, Cicero and Quintilian.

It is not surprising, therefore, that the education of talented youth in the second century became a matter of public concern, and that the municipalities in Italy and the provinces undertook the financial subsidy of their schools of grammar and rhetoric as well as their teachers. Most of the early Latin Christian fathers were trained in this discipline. Saint Augustine was a student of rhetoric at Carthage and a professor at Milan. Ausonius at Bordeaux in the fourth century and Sidonius at Lyons in the fifth were the latest examples of the persistence of Quintilian's legacy. Both were Christians, the latter a bishop and subsequently sainted; yet they exhibit a remarkable ability to mix the sacred with the profane and to rub shoulders, as it were, in a friendly and graceful fashion, with their non-Christian schoolfellows and neighbors.

From the fall of the western empire to Charlemagne, however, the issues were the cultural unity of Europe itself and the very survival of the Latin language as a medium of communication, literary and administrative. By the beginning of the fifth century Christianity was supreme, and the bishop was sitting in the seat of the older municipal magistrates. Learning was being transferred from the urban school to the monastery and public power from the civil to the ecclesiastical authority. It was now the task of the Roman church to assume the burden of Vergil's imperative, *Tu regere imperio populos, Romane, memento.* It was no accident that the Roman Empire and the Roman Catholic church were the only two institutions in western Christendom that combined a conviction of a special divine mission with a claim to universal dominion. The issue was no longer the survival of literary Latin; it was the survival of Latin, any kind of Latin, so long as it was intelligible, barbarisms and solecisms included. In the eighth century Saint Boniface, when he heard a child being baptized *in nomine Patria et Filia et Spiritu Sancta,* was genuinely concerned whether the baptism was valid. In the previous century Gregory the Great had come to the conclusion that the church had absorbed from the pagan classics all the culture that it needed, and he rebuked Bishop Desiderius of Vienne for teaching

Christian boys the pagan classics. He had Prudentius, he said, and he did not need Ovid: "The same lips cannot sing the praises of Jove and Christ." For quite a while the issue was by no means sure, and it was only with Charlemagne, who lifted up the fallen diadem and once again assumed the imperial mantle, that the dawn broke.

The story of the revival of learning is too well known to be recounted in any detail here. It began with Bede at Jarrow and Alcuin at York, and with the latter passed from England to the Continent when Charlemagne founded his palace school at Aix-la-Chapelle. The process that started in the Dark Ages was now being reversed. The care of learning was being moved from the monastery back to the town and its superintendence from the bishop to the crown. Since *externi* were now admitted to the new schools, the first small step toward the secularization of learning had been taken. Although education remained completely under the ecclesiastical thumb, it was now possible for men who did not envisage a career in the church to seek a higher education.

The purposes of this new curriculum were at first purely utilitarian: (1) to train priests who could read the Latin Bible; (2) to provide scholars who could read Latin to pursue the study of philosophy and theology; (3) to secure bishops who could keep records in Latin and thus efficiently administer a diocese; and finally, (4) to educate laymen in Latin so that they could become trained civil servants and administer the law. Thus medieval Latin emerged. It was not the Latin of Cicero, but at all events it was Latin and, under the best circumstances, as with the later Scholastics, correct and precise Latin suited to the needs of the time.

The next change in the cultural complexion of Europe occurred between the death of Charlemagne and the beginning of the thirteenth century. The causes of this change were many, but important were the revival of trade, the renewal of town life, and the rise to prominence, if not to power, of a new middle class. The medieval university came into being, and with it the development of graduate specialties: (1) philosophy, and especially logic; (2) theology, and with it the move to reconcile Aristotle (and to a lesser degree, Plato) with Christian revelation; (3) law, especially Roman law, and with it the need to read and study the Justinian corpus; and finally, (4) medicine, with attention first to Galen and subsequently to Hippocrates. Thus arose in the medieval university the higher faculties of philosophy, theology, law, and medicine. Together with these developments, there occurred subtle changes in attitude. The prayers of Saint Augustine *credo quia incredibile est* and *credo, Domine, adjuva incredulitatem meam* gave way to Anselm's affirmation *credo ut intellegam*. It was no longer *intellectus quaerens fidem* but *fides quaerens intellectum*. Philosophy became the handmaid of theology, and revelation was viewed as the friend and not the foe of the rational soul. The second change in attitude was the conscious search for and evenutal recovery of the Greco-Roman classical sense of civic virtue to replace, or at any rate to exist alongside of, the practice of Christian perfection. The rise of the cathedral schools encouraged these changes. In the first place, they were conveniently located in the larger urban centers, especially for the attendance of the new middle class; and in the second place, they welcomed *externi* who had no intention of becoming monks or priests.

The third change in attitude was the development of a certain worldliness and a search for creature comforts, as the spiritual manuals put it. Luxuries became available, even if only to a limited degree, and with luxuries leisure, and with leisure the pursuit of pleasure and, particularly, the joys of mundane love. Naturally, together with all this there developed a certain bourgeois cynicism with respect to the merits and practices of the religious life. No wonder that Ovid and Juvenal began to enjoy a vogue! The new men had no need of Prudentius—they had Ovid. It was in such an environment that the vernacular languages began to acquire literary maturity in the hands of such artists as Dante in Italy and Chaucer in England. A counterculture was in process of growth.

Once, however, the new men decided to abandon medieval ways, they had no choice but to return to antiquity. Just as the men of the Reformation sought to recover primitive Christianity, so the men of the Renaissance tried to find in the secular culture of classical antiquity a substitute for the obscurantism of the Middle Ages. Latin was the only universal learned language in western Europe, and any formal education was of necessity in and through the Latin language. Greek, to be sure, came in as an adjunct to Latin, but not as the language of academic discourse and instruction. Second, the medieval church was the only universal institution in western Europe in the sixteenth century that had at hand the organization and facilities to undertake formal education. Therefore, the new education, however much it might seek its models in the glory that was Greece and the grandeur that was Rome, remained under the supervision and discipline of the Christian ecclesiastical authorities. Thus the nuptials between classicism and Christianity were celebrated, and the union was consummated.

It is instructive to recall how clearly and surely the men who did this knew what they were doing. Erasmus maintained that the profane subjects of the classics were admissible only *si propter Christum*. Ignatius inverted this proposition by saying that one should absorb along with his letters the morals of a Christian. Thus the *bonus vir dicendi peritus* of Isocrates becomes the *bonus vir scribendi peritus* of Cicero and Quintilian and finally the *bonus vir vivendi peritus* of Christian humanism. It is also instructive to recall how long into modern times this partnership lasted. In 1639 the words of a contemporary letter were carved on the gates of Harvard College. It read: "After God had carried us safe to New England and we had builded our houses, provided necessaries for our livelihood, reared convenient places for God's worship, and settled the civil government: one of the next things we longed for and looked after, was to advance learning and to perpetuate it to posterity, dreading to leave an illiterate ministry to the Churches, when our present ministers shall lie in the dust." When King's College, later Columbia University, was opened in New York City in 1754, the advertisement read: "The chief thing that is aimed at in this college, is to teach and engage the children to know God in Jesus Christ, and to love and serve Him in all sobriety, godliness, and richness of life, with a perfect heart and a willing mind; and to train them up in all virtuous habits and all such useful knowledge as may render them creditable to their families and friends, ornaments to their country, and useful to the public weal in their generation." It was not until 1852 that those who were not members of the Church of England could stand for degrees at Oxford, and not until 1876 that they could hold fellowships. Thus the classical curriculum became and remained Christian, and the propaedeutic Christian education became and remained classical.

It remains to inquire what purposes this Renaissance

education served then and up to the days of my youth. In the first place, in early modern times it was the necessary prerequisite for all higher education, in law, in medicine, and preeminently in the church. This was particularly true of the Roman Catholic church, for which Latin was the one and only language of ritual and administration; but also, in the Protestant churches Latin was required for the study of philosophy, theology, and sacred scripture. As to law, in England Latin was not necessary for the study of the English common law, where the Inns of Court sufficed; but on the Continent it was indispensable for the pursuit of the civil law, for which the Code of Justinian was required. Most important of all, the classical curriculum provided the terminal education for those who did not seek further professional instruction. For them, the classical curriculum provided not only the necessary discipline in the use of language in writing and conversation but also an acquaintance with the cultural background of European thought and morals and the necessary social graces to be at ease in an aristocratic milieu. In short, a classical education became the badge of civility, and a knowledge of Latin a sign of that quality which Pascal calls the *ésprit de finesse.* It was the *enkuklios paideia,* the *liberalis disciplina,* the all-around education of that limited group whose destiny was to give orders, whether in the churches, in the parliaments, in the officer class in the armed service, in the professions of law and medicine, or finally, in trade and business. Superficially, the classical curriculum seems to have been a kind of initiation ceremony whereby those who belonged to the ruling classes preserved their own cultural continuity and provided a kind of trial by intellectual ordeal whereby those who did not belong were enabled—a few of them by hard work, good luck, and winning scholarships by passing difficult examinations—to achieve admission to the upper echelon. But this is not the whole story. For all its faults, its selectivity, its exclusiveness, its effortless superiority, one might even say its arrogance, the classical curriculum under Christian auspices was until 1914 the only remaining badge of European unity. Sir Edward Grey knew it on that early August morning in 1914; Hilaire Belloc expressed it when he wrote: "Europe is the faith and the faith is Europe, and the decline of the faith is the decline of Europe." Shortly after the close of World War I, Jean Renoir dramatized it in that most sensitive and perceptive film entitled *The Grand Illusion*. The British officer with his swagger stick, the French officer with his white gloves, and the German officer with his monocle, all killed one another off in Flanders fields and at Verdun. *Requiescant in pace!*

Now, what has happened to the classics since 1914? In the first place, the Christian churches, including the Roman Catholic church, are no longer in control of education; in fact, they are no longer in control. They have abdicated their position of authority; they no longer give orders—not even the Pope of Rome. The classes in control are no longer Christian except in name. I do not mean that there are not professing and indeed genuinely sincere Christians among them, but simply that their public decisions are not now made on the basis of Christian morality—and this is the whole point. The Christian churches have been succeeded in the position of authority by two new classes: the managerial class, whose principle is efficiency; and the technological class, whose principle is material progress. Before neither tribunal can there be an appeal to mercy. Thus, the Christian pillar upon which our humanistic education rested is no longer there. We are no longer a Christian nation, and this opinion has recently been supported by several decisions of the United States Supreme Court.

In the second place, the arts college has been destroyed by mass education. The classical curriculum never was, and was never intended to be, an education for the many. This is a hard saying, but it must be said because it is true. The Christian classical culture was based on the hypothesis that seems to me to have been universal among advanced societies until now: namely, that the ruling class first disciplines itself from within and then, having done so, disciplines the lower orders from without. It occurred to me, while watching the growth of communism, that the discipline that the Communist élite (the party members) imposed upon themselves resembled nothing so much as the discipline that the Jesuit order imposed upon its members in the period of its greatest success. The purpose of the classical curriculum—and once again may I emphasize that it reached its highest expression in the small church-related liberal arts college—was to train a Christian élite. A Christian élite no longer exists, so far, at any rate, as it exercises public power.

In the third place, mass education has removed the arts college from the center of the campus to its periphery. We now have colleges of education, colleges of commerce, colleges of public administration, and so forth—all on the undergraduate level. But the purpose of these colleges is not the inculcation of a way of life but professional training either to do a particular job or to make a specific kind of thing. They are in effect training schools, and the only point on which they differ from the earlier plebeian training school is that they transcend the manual level.

Finally, the arts college has been given the coup de

grâce by the descent upon it from above of the graduate
school, particularly in those subjects that once were
the germane property of the arts college. This development was a contribution of German scholarship to the
higher learning that reached American universities
roughly at the beginning of the present century but had
barely touched Oxford when I began my studies there.
Now, there was nothing wrong in this development in
itself. It was the application of the principles and techniques of the higher learning to the traditional subjects
of the arts college, particularly to Latin, Greek, and the
study of literature in general. It has produced a body of
knowledge that has immensely broadened and deepened
our appreciation of classical antiquity. No teacher of
the classics, even in the traditional arts college, should
be unacquainted with it. But this is not to say that it
should affect the arts college so that practical and professional excellence in arts college subjects becomes the
aim of undergraduate education. This deviation from
the earlier norm is particularly apparent in the study
of the modern languages. It is one thing to teach a
student to read French; another to train him to speak
it. In the first instance the purpose is to equip him to
become culturally acquainted with a great literature;
in the second instance the purpose is to provide him
with a facile and current vocabulary for practical conversational usage. The one does not necessarily imply
the other, as I discovered when I first visited Paris as a
young man. On the other hand, an unlettered alien can
come to our shores and in a short time acquire a practical conversational facility in English—not the best
English, to be sure, simply *parlando*. But this tendency
toward practicability and professionalization is evident
in subjects other than the modern languages, among
them Latin, Greek, and ancient history. Too many of

our students today study the classics to the end that they become professors of the classics, and by doing so evade or at least make secondary the acquisition of a humanistic manner of life. We must not forget what Stephen Leacock said in his little essay on "Homer and Humbug": "I know there are solid arguments advanced in favor of the classics. I often hear them from my colleagues. My friend the professor of Greek tells me that he truly believes the classics have made him what he is. This is a very grave statement, if well founded." When graduate disciplines are brought down to the undergraduate level, *Wissenschaft* triumphs over *humanitas.*

This professionalization and specialization within the classical disciplines has had another effect upon undergraduate teaching. It has limited the instructional ambit of the teacher. One no longer teaches ancient history. One teaches Greek history; another teaches Roman history; and a third teaches the history of the ancient Near East. One no longer teaches the classics. One teaches Latin; another teaches Greek. Once again, this fragmentation of special interest is appropriate in the graduate school, although even there I think it is overdone. Surely it is out of place, or at any rate unnecessary, in undergraduate teaching. In my own student days the same man who taught Homer in Greek also taught Vergil in Latin and Milton in English, passing from one language to another and from one poet to another with all the ease and insouciance of the amateur. In fact, that is what he was—an amateur—and that is what he ought to have been. *Amateur* comes from *amo*, "I love," and he loved what he was teaching; he loved his pupils too, and they loved him in turn. An amateur pursues a subject, whether it is contract bridge, or chess, or tennis, or Latin, or English poetry, because it is fun and he enjoys it. Ignatius saw this, and the *Ratio* recommends that a boy should pursue his studies *cum animi hilaritate,* laughing and joking on the way. Looking back upon my own academic life, I have come to the conclusion that perhaps my greatest achievement has been that I have been able to perform my professional duties and at the same time maintain my amateur status.

This brings us to our last two questions. What is humanism? And can we preserve humanism without the classical curriculum and the Christian dispensation that have supported it for so long a time? With regard to the first question, no precise definition can be given. Humanism is like love—it must be experienced to be appreciated. On the other hand, its nature is not ineffable. Perhaps it can best be defined in negative terms. For instance, political science teaches us much, but it cannot teach us that the good shepherd gives his life for his sheep. The study of economics teaches us much, but it cannot teach us that it is more blessed to give than to receive. Modern medicine can teach us much, but it cannot teach us that it is the duty of the strong to protect the weak. These are eternal verities, however much honest men may disagree with regard to their particular application. We all know that sympathy is better than callousness; that mercy is better than justice; that humility is better than arrogance; and that continence is better than self-indulgence.

This is only another way of saying that the purpose of a humanistic education is the training of the emotions. In this argument we have the Franciscans and the Augustinians on our side against the Thomists. Scotus tells us that the will is greater than the intellect, and Thomas à Kempis that it is better to love the Trinity than to be able to define it. We also have the men of the Renaissance on our side. Petrarch states that it is better to will the good than to know the truth. We also have the great mystics on our side. William Blake says that the forgiveness of sins is the essence of Christianity. The emotions are strange affections of the human soul. They are deepened and widened by repeated experience and at the same time corrupted by overindulgence. This makes their training a delicate discipline. Love feeds on itself, but it can be sated. As both Plato and Aristotle taught, the good man is the man whose emotions are sharpened to the razor's edge but remain in accord with right reason. In short, the ultimate purpose of the arts college is moral rectitude softened by love and pity. In the words of Pascal, the heart hath its reasons of which the reason knoweth nothing.

What then do we have left—humanism standing erect upon nothing, but humanism still standing, as the young are now showing us, however confused their thoughts may be and however faltering their words. *Ex ore infantium!* Fortunately, humanism never was and never can be a Christian classical monopoly. It is part of human nature, and all men partake of it to a greater or lesser degree. *Homo sum: humani nihil a me alienum puto.* Moreover, there have been and are other forms of humanism than ours—Chinese, Indian, Islamic, and Jewish, to mention some. But it is one thing to have individuals who are humane and quite another thing to have an established humanistic culture based upon an educational system and discipline. Our crisis is that our humanism has been founded upon half a millennium of conscious, organized, disciplined education based upon the Greek and Roman classics and the Christian faith. Moreover, we have tied our mores to an absolute. We have had no Confucius to teach us the prudential virtues. Consequently, when the Christian faith collapses, Christian morals, which are our mores, collapse with them.

This can be catastrophic. *Ave atque vale! Morituri te salutamus!*

Watchman, then, what of the night? This side of complete chaos—and that can happen, read Gregory of Tours—I see three possibilities: (1) In the course of time, *in saeculis saeculorum,* our Christian classic culture may be subsumed, as the philosophers say, by an alien dispensation, Chinese, Indian, Islamic or some other, just as the Christian culture subsumed that of the Greco-Roman world. *Non uno itinere itur ad tam grande mysterium,* as Symmachus, the last of the pagans, said when in the fourth century he protested against the removal of the statue of Victory from the Roman senate chamber. There is no one only way to the ultimate mystery. However, when we reflect that it took Christian Europe a thousand years to achieve this kind of synthesis, such an anticipation is not immediately consoling, and it is doubtful that any of us living today will survive to witness the event. (2) Another way might be through the medium of the fine arts: painting, sculpture, music, the theater, and such like. The *Ratio* itself says: *friget enim poesis sine theatro.* The Muse of poetry needs the theater for her life-blood. This alternative has at least one advantage over the classical curriculum: it can be made to reach the many in a way and to a degree that the old discipline never did, and it is the many and the young that must be reached. They are already crowding the schools and universities; they have already moved the arts from the fashionable drawing room to the street and the marketplace, and they are no longer content to spend their lives as Plutarch's "rude, mechanical multitude." (3) Finally, there is the suggestion made recently in the pages of the *Times Literary Supplement* (London) by Professor F. R. Leavis and by Roy Fuller, the present Professor of Poetry at Oxford. Conceding (*non sine lacrimis*) the end of the old system, they recommend that the English School—or, as we say, the English Department—assume the mantle of humanism. After all, just as Latin in the time of Quintilian and into the Renaissance had displaced the Greek of Cicero's period and had become the literary language of the learned world, so by this time the several vernacular languages (and for us this means English) have achieved literary maturity and are in the position to displace Latin as the language of polite discourse and instruction. None will deny that they—and preeminently the English language, if one thinks of Chaucer, Shakespeare, and Milton—have within themselves the essence and all the qualities of humanism. This alternative appeals to me because it leaves something for us classicists to do. Just as, until now, we have been explaining classical mythology to Christian humanists, so, hereafter, we can explain Christian mythology to the new secular humanists. *Non omnis moriar.*

In the entire span of recorded history there have been three ultimate dangers to the survival of advanced societies: undisciplined power; undisciplined wealth; and undisciplined pleasure. The onset of one alone would be difficult enough to offset; the attack of all three marching abreast is terrorizing. Surely, Plato must have had a point when he said that only those should be trusted with authority who could be counted upon to refuse it. *Nolo episcopari.* Surely Saint Francis must have known what he was doing when he embraced Lady Poverty. Surely John Calvin could not have been wholly wrong when he taught that only those are to be trusted with great wealth who have been rigorously trained from early childhood "to shun delights and live laborious days." It is time, therefore, that we recall some of the maxims of the classical past: *meden agan, ne quid nimis,* nothing too much; *gnothi seauton,* know thyself. "The proper study of mankind is man." To the humanist the universe is anthropocentric. He may be wrong. It may not be. But it is the only assumption that makes the human condition tolerable. Protagoras said that there are many appearances and some are better than others, but none is truer. Among the phenomena is the phenomenon of Man. Art is long, but life is short. There is the famous passage in Herodotus where Xerxes, watching his immense host crossing the Hellespont, bursts out weeping and, when asked why, replies that it has just occurred to him that none of these men will be alive a hundred years from now. *Sunt lacrimae rerum.* As Mr. Dooley, the sage of Halsted Street, said: "I know histhry isn't true, Hinnissy, because it ain't like what I see every day in Halsted Street. If any man comes along with a histhry of Greece or Rome that'll show me the people fightin', gettin' dhrunk, makin' love, gettin' married, owin' the grocery man, an' bein' without hard coal, I'd believe there was a Greece and Rome, but not before. . . . Histhry is a post-mortem examination. It tells you what a counthry died iv. But I would like to know what it lived iv." Perhaps what the children mean when they say today that love is better than war—though they do not know this because since they are not products of Christian classicism—is that the Greek word for human excellence, *arete,* should be sublimated to the Christian concept of human perfection, *agape.*

by David F. Heimann

Christian Humanism
in the Fourth Century: Saint Jerome

In the history of the confrontation between the cultural
forms of classical antiquity and the growing influence
of the Gospel, the concept of Christian humanism
is frequently presented as the combination of the best
that each had to offer to the civilizing of the Western world. There are obvious and very sound reasons
behind this choice. Humanism has always seemed a
most natural choice of word for describing whatever
elements characterized the cultural refinement of the
classical spirit at its best, and Christian, as a specific
form of humanism, asserts that it is in the Christian
view of man that humanism reaches its happiest development.

There are problems in using these words, as well.
The concept of Christian humanism is, historically, more
regularly applied to a much later era, the late Middle
Ages or the Renaissance, an age that evolved a far
fuller picture of the role of man within the Christian
scheme of things. This is not to say that the role of man
is, by its nature, uncongenial or wanting to the Christian
point of view. However, it is possible that a scholar who
looks closely at the fourth century might conclude that
the Christian philosophy had not yet evolved its philos-

ophy of man to the point where it could add significantly to pagan humanism.

One must in fact observe that the two elements, *Christian* and *humanism*, do not always articulate perfectly: too often they contradict each other in areas where actually there was the raw stuff of an eventual synthesis that could have promoted the most cherished objectives of each element.

One difficulty arises from the fact that the application of the terms *Christian* and *humanism* to the fourth century involves some extrapolation. The terms are carried back over several centuries of development, and what the Christian humanist's view of the world must have been after Dante is, to some degree, predicated upon what it could have been only *in potentia* in the fourth century.

Definitions

The problem can be approached by two kinds of definition. The first is in terms of essence. Humanism is essentially the philosophy that proclaims the central importance of the role played by man, and Christian, broadly speaking, means pertaining to, or characterized by, the philosophy of the Gospel.

What is really needed, however, is not so much a simple definition in terms of essence as a phenomenological approximation of the concepts involved, an awareness of the range of meaning gradually appropriated by the terms, and determined ultimately by the historical circumstances in which they developed and the peculiar limitations of the broader areas to which historically they have been applied. Thus *Christian* must be distinguished into denominatively Christian and historically Christian; *humanism* into the Renaissance culture we know by that name, with the rediscovered human values it sought to assert, and what is more denominatively humanistic, that is, the exaltation of the role of man. There are those who could not possibly admit the term *Christian humanism* as applied to the fourth century in any conceivable frame of reference. *Christian* here is not the Christian of Apostolic or sub-Apostolic times. It is Roman Christianity, in some respects more a cultural milieu than a spiritual challenge, yet still demanding fresh impetus for its Gospel. At the same time, it is not the Christianity of our own day with all its dogma well worked out.

In much the same way it is indeed probable that the humanism of fifth-century Athens could claim logically to exclude the very notion of a Christian humanism, for, by definition, the "intellectual search for and interest in the true nature of man" [1] is inherently opposed to either enlightenment from a god or the eventual reduction of human effort to an ancillary status vis-à-vis the divine. Historically, this rigorous application of the terms has generally been avoided. Humanism can equally well apply to the philosophy that asserts the primacy of the human role in a universe in which there are gods, or in which there is a God. The first chapter of Genesis, for example, is a bold though essentially preliminary step toward the exaltation and liberation of man from the superstitious fear of gods and demons and existential insecurities of every kind, yet it is set squarely in a theocentric context. The same is true of belief in an afterlife. It can free a man for further concentration on the dignity of his human role just as well as it can violate what might be claimed to be the philosophical limitations of humanism: man must be left to his own resources. In a word, there is nothing in the belief in a divinity, per se, to exclude the harmonious linking of the two terms under consideration. Humanism can ideally be Christian, and Christianity can, in principle, be humanistic.

There have been, moreover, changes in the meaning of the key concepts. Thus, a Christian humanism without the external trappings and modes of thought proper to the Renaissance would be inconceivable from one point of view, no matter how secondary some of these elements might actually be to an essential definition of either humanism or Christianity. This is the precaution with which we must approach a consideration of the historical hallmarks of humanism: concern with man, with letters, with the past, with a classical ideal for art and society that is meant to be largely normative, and with the objectives and ideals of what we have come to know as liberal or humane education.

So much for the historically determined definition. From another point of view it is more important to examine the essential definition of the terms. For then one can not only get at the fundamental elements but one can look back into history to identify the first appearances of trends or attitudes or spirit that can be recognized as denominative elements of Christian humanism. We are thus ultimately forced into the position of using terms that have become overgrown with layers of meaning, while ourselves distinguishing the basic definitions. How humanistic and how Christian, then, is the Christian humanism of the fourth century?

Another essential in the search for a definition is a measure of contemporaneity. This involves something of a reconstruction, similar to the methods of biblical studies, where the emphasis has rightly been upon recapturing the original spirit of the books. Our interpretation here should achieve a sympathetic appreciation of the world views of antiquity. There exists as yet, for ex-

ample, no convincing appreciation of the Christian outlook, in all its nobility and essential limitations, that
animates Jerome's *Lives of the Desert Fathers*, or the
early Christian dialogues; again, scholars have not yet
properly identified the tone and spirit within the many
patristic letters of the Christian martyrologies. Augustine's *Confessions* and *City of God* have been approached in this more sympathetic way, as being docu-
ments that have early made their way into the larger
framework of world literature; but many elements need
to be considered before our evaluation is wholly in keeping with the thinking of the fourth century itself, and
not simply an overlay of later scholarship. Too often,
for example, we steal a page from the Fathers themselves and read their works simply as mines of dogma.
We should do much better to look into them for a view
of the world and of man's position within it.

Classical Humanism

Classical humanism, in this context, describes a vision
whose horizons are set by a paramount concern for the
human, for the ideal of man and humanity as capable
of individual and collective realization. Its hallmarks
are proportion, harmony, balance, and aesthetic appreciation of the most noble elements in man (not excepting the areas where human experience impinges upon
the otherworldly), all inspired by a fine sense of form
molded to mate with and perfectly to express the content of the vision. This is an ideal slow to develop, and
once it is achieved, both in classical Greece and later
again in classical Rome, it rapidly disintegrates.

Hence the need for the well-known distinction between classical and antique.[2] *Classical* refers to that
whole nobility of human vision and ideals that has

ever caught the fancy of every true lover of the human. The age that succeeds upon the breakup of the classical may be, however, more properly referred to as *antique.* It is characterized by the retention of much of the external forms of the classical, but little if any of the spirit that gave life to that form; by a growing preoccupation with erudition versus creativity; and by a corresponding lack of political, social, and cultural sense of direction. The true flowering of the classical soul, an intense but quickly dissipating vision, considerably antedates the triumph of the Christian philosophy, with which it never did come into direct contact.

One likes to make the case that all that was best in Greek and Roman thought was channeled directly into Christianity, just as in another context one would like to envision the stream of Christian revelation running in one continuous flow from Old to New Testaments. The picture is not so simple as that. It is the antique and not the classical culture that meets with Christianity in its early years when Christianity was in a position to build a true continuity with the traditions of Rome. What Christianity takes, or even could take, of the antique past is, moreover, not the better elements. From Vergil, for example, the antique culture drew grammar and divination, but its entire literary orientation was everywhere too dependent upon compendia and commonplace, dogmatic misinformation joined with a triteness and a pervading sense of form that had already grown sterile when it no longer functioned as the form of classical harmony. This is a distinction frequently enough made, but not always borne in mind. Historically, the result is a breach of continuity: there cannot ever be that happy and all but unnoticed transition from classical humanism to Christian humanism. To ask, in fact, what would have ensued had Christian philosophy been wedded with the ripeness of the classical glory is, in some respects, quite pointless. From another point of view, however, it is a very healthy question, for its very phrasing points up much that deserves attention in the less than ideal state of things that actually obtained.

Although it is important to be aware of this far-reaching distinction between classical and antique, one must not overstate the position. The total historical configuration that was classical humanism does not, when it begins to dissipate, simply burst like a bubble. There are elements in the dissolution that survive for a later regrouping in the Christian culture. There is thus a partial continuity, the continuity of individual elements within the larger discontinuity of an interrupted tradition. There is still access to the classical humanistic ideals, but now it involves, much as it does in the Renaissance or in modern times, a rediscovery; and the techniques for managing this rediscovery, this restoration of formal continuity with the past, were not in the fourth century so sophisticated or reliable as they are today.

Christianity was, moreover, already well on the road to evolving its own culture and philosophy. As a result, the less than accurate recovery of the older humanistic ideals proves to be something of an advantage in one sense, in that it affords the Christian development greater scope to assert those elements that are peculiarly Christian and still label the results as classical. Part of the Christian development, after all, ought to be what it can draw from the humanism of ages past. However, here the fact of discontinuity, especially when it is not clearly recognized, does invite considerable distortion. When all is said and done, one must admit that the classical spirit as a total outlook upon life had grown so alien that only a few could lay valid claim to the sympathetic understanding of even its broader outlines, and fewer still could make a contribution toward its effective continuation.

The concepts of continuity and discontinuity, which provide a convenient polarization for studying the debt of Christian humanism in the fourth century to the classical heritage, have led to many conclusions, some of which need to be reexamined. Time being a continuum for the experience of the individual, the scholar likes to superimpose a temporal sequence upon the flux of the centuries and find evidence of continuity or discontinuity at every turn, the seeds of one thing or the *Fortleben* of something else. In this the scholar deserves our thanks; but to deserve our praise, he must be thorough. There is great danger that he will wrongly lead us to accept a basically incomplete statement of the reality whose outlines he means to trace. Notwithstanding these dangers, there must be a thorough examination of the characteristic elements of humanism, and their historical developments and adaptations, before we can even consider the validity of a Christian humanism in the fourth century.

Man

The humanist is expected to have a coherent picture of the central position occupied by man in the scheme of things. The pagan had this in the classical past, but it was a lesser ingredient in the antique culture inherited by the fourth century. The central picture of man, in the Christian theory, was also enunciated, in Scripture and in the earliest Christian preaching. The Christian, in pursuing his ideals, might logically incorporate the humanism of the classical past.

The humanist picture is supposed to flow from the consideration of man and his nature. The Christian picture of man, on the other hand, is supposed to flow from the dignity of man envisioned as the citizen of two worlds, an ideal illustrated by the Incarnation. Thus the Christian humanist view of man must harmoniously blend two world pictures. We shall see shortly that whereas Christ and the Christian myth should, and perhaps could, have effected this amalgam, de facto it did not. The Christian paradox was potentially a definitive insight but seldom a true fusion of the two, often rival, claims upon human allegiance.

The story of fourth-century humanism is further complicated by the fact that pagan humanism looks solely to human reason for its knowledge of the philosophy of man, whereas Christian philosophy purports to draw upon a revelation as well. Thus it appears to conceal its debt to Greek philosophy, as transmitted by Cicero and others who had learned its essential modes of thought and divisions, and also to the pagan view of human dignity that is fundamental to the humanist tradition. It is shortsighted to regard all these continuing or rediscovered insights as purely the product of Christian philosophy.

Letters

The humanist turns habitually to literature and the arts as an abiding and readily accessible source for the contemplation of his ideals of human dignity and endeavor. This conservative attitude has always demanded that the models that the humanist admires should have survived several generations; here the Christian humanist draws his conservatism from the Roman sense of tradition as well as his own inherent religious tendencies. The humanist tends to call these works *classics*, in the sense that having stood the test of time they can present their insights to each succeeding generation as sources universally relevant to every age. The culture of the past is thus applied to the enlightenment of the present; its ideals and criteria are canonized, invested with normative value as models toward which any contemporary humanism must necessarily aspire.

The Roman vocabulary uses the same word, *mores*, to describe both what has always obtained and what is the proper standard of any human behavior. The Christian develops this identification further in his discovery of a providential continuity in the economy of revelation whereby God wills that the truths and ideals achieved by ages past should serve as building blocks for an increasingly lofty and definitive stage of spiritual and intellectual development. This attitude is further reinforced by the Roman tradition of continuity within a literary genre, and its extension to the world of early Christian literary endeavor.

Language

Historically the humanist has developed a nice sense of language if only because of his involvement with the literary records of the past. It is his capacity for speech that makes the human specifically different from the beast, and the Roman word for culture in general, *humanitas*, has always represented the Roman ideal of the fullest development of those qualities that are most human in man. In this context the proper definition and use of words and language have always been regarded as a convenient and accurate index of human intelligence.

This is more than simple fascination or *jeu d'esprit*

in the true humanist who should display a keen appreciation of the need for formal equivalence between the truth that he apprehends in his mind and its eventual verbal or written expression. This is never simply a quest for elegance and polish, but, as it were, an attempt to establish a sort of inner harmony between the world of ideas and the world of verbal expression. The ensuing discipline of expression tests the depth and accuracy of his thinking (if only in that the expression involves considerable time and effort) and exerts a powerful semantic control over the likelihood of either the verbal expression or the intellectual concept ever being lightly abandoned. The one mutually complements and reinforces the other.

The Latin language is especially adapted to achieve this nicety and harmony of expression. The very forging of the Latin literary language and style, as a matter of fact, involved generations of dedicated and earnest labor in warring with the medium of language. These efforts are, to be sure, characteristic of all artistic development, but the course that the Latin literary language took was also influenced by Greek literary forms and models, the *exemplaria* that animated and inspired the Roman effort. The result was the fine balance and sense of language that marked the *humanitas* of Cicero and the artistry of expression of the poetry of the Golden Age—two precious ideals in the heritage that Rome left to the early Christian centuries.

The Latin literary tradition thus developed a special predilection for polite (that is, polished) diction; for *emendatio* (the painstaking elimination of every imperfection); for *lucidus ordo* (clearly grasped meaning supported and set off by elegant diction); for *callida iunctura* (effective and ingenious ordering and arrangement of words to enhance their basic functions and nuance). This is a noble tradition that, once proclaimed, never really dies. The techniques forged by the need for expression remained available, like many other forms that have outlived their basic inspiration, for emulation by later generations of Latin writers who, though lacking the literary vision and potential of the Golden Age, found the ideal at least partially achievable in their careful attention to the smaller details of composition.

The structure of the Latin literary language is such that it can express infinitely more in the way of subtle antithesis through its flexible word order than, for example, can modern English. Contrasting words like *one-many, you-me, up-down,* can, in the more flexible structure of the Latin sentence, be set side by side or otherwise stressed and contrasted. The Christian vocabulary is by its very nature full of such contrasted themes: paradox that life is death, or death life. The Latin Christian authors exploit this potential to the full.

Rediscovery

Humanism can involve something of a rediscovery, in the Renaissance sense of the word, even where we would not look for it as essential. This accounts for much of its vitality. Even in classical Roman times this element was never wholly lacking (cf. Horace's *exemplaria Graeca*), and in the fourth century it is much in evidence. It implies essentially two things: enough continuity with the humanist tradition to create a sympathetic atmosphere, and enough discontinuity to make the realization of the humanist insights a more or less new discovery for that age, thereby providing for development and change within areas that would otherwise have been too rigidly controlled by the conservative force of tradition.

There is no compelling reason why the Christian faith and the Christian philosophy should not have developed a humanism that successfully emulated and continued the best elements of the classical past, despite the existence of differences in emphasis within the Christian humanist's attitude toward man, the classical past, letters and language, and in the degree of conscious rediscovery that he was able and willing to aspire to. It is disappointing to note that Christian humanism fails to achieve its fullest potential in all these respects; yet it is gratifying to observe how aware Christian thinkers had become to at least some of these considerations.

The Christian Myth

The philosophy that animates the Christian synthesis involves continuity with the humanistic culture of the past. Although it is true that Christian thinkers very clearly began turning to the philosophies of Greece and Rome for models along which to develop the Christian message, it is also true that not all these philosophies were humanistic.

Still, the Christian world picture or the Christian myth (that is, those elements in Christian thinking and revelation that correspond to *mythos* in antiquity) is characterized primarily by a radical unity and total depth. First of all, the Christian philosophy effectively subsumes the fundamentals of Greek and Roman philosophy: the vision of Plato, a world of pure and perfect existences whose shadows only are what we encounter in the life of the senses; the logical necessity of what was recalled of the Aristotelian system; the contemplative charm of Neo-Platonic gradations to divinity; the individual and personal imperatives of an afterlife, an ideal proposed and promoted by the mystery religions; and the Stoic gospel as a moral imperative. All these strains eventually find their place in the vision of a God who is both creator and object of love and guarantee of the soul's individual immortality.

The Christian synthesis also bridged a deeper gap. Roman religion had sought primarily to achieve and maintain the *pax deorum* by a ritualized observance of all the externals of the divine cult, devoid of individual moral commitment to the Olympian divinities or even to the native Roman deities. There was no necessary connection between the gods' blessing upon the Roman state and the private morality of its citizens. In equating the two as equally imperative elements of religious observance, the Christian philosophy achieved a phenomenon unique in antiquity and a source of interior strength.

The person of Jesus Christ serves as key to this remarkable accomplishment. As the embodiment of the Christian *mythos*, he combines heaven and earth, divinity and humanity. At the same time, he exists as the Person Christ and the Mystical Christ, the whole body of the Christian Church who believe in his Gospel and are raised by his grace to a higher, supernatural level of existence on condition of their being one with him. In a single stroke Christianity might thus answer all the enigmas that Greek and Roman *mythos* might appear to raise: it might assert the value and dignity of man and still safeguard the prerogatives of divinity; it might settle the divergent claims of *heros* and *theos*, while asserting the unity of mankind, the purpose of human existence in harmony with a divine will, free will and foreknowledge in God—Christ as all in all.

Whereas the ancient humanisms had tended to look upon man as the measure of all things, this was not a view with which Christianity was particularly sympathetic. Logically it might well have been, for humanity was given new status through the advent of the *novus Adam*, the new man who incorporated heaven and earth in the unified expression of the human dilemma, by virtue of which he could truly be called the measure of all things. This conception could have been called Christian humanism from one point of view: the philosophy developed about the concept of *the* man, Christ. It is not, however, what Christian humanism should have come to mean, and at all events it certainly does not characterize the thought of the fourth century, when the very word humanity, *humanitas*, tended to express one extreme of a polarization, *divinitas* being the other extreme, and thereby to become a pejorative concept rather than the Roman term for culture. By the fourth century, the role of man as the measure of all things, although consistent with the basic principles of the Christian *mythos*, had already suffered considerable distortion.

Religious Continuity

For the more obvious continuities within the religious philosophy of antique Rome we can look to much of the form, the liturgical ritual and dignity (*gravitas*) that marked Roman religion: the liturgical season and its adaptations of the pagan vegetal cycle and hero cults; the concept of an initiate body of elect within the larger mass of lesser mortals; the derivation of personal standards of morality from an ethical philosophy based on an idealized yet coherent conception of the nature of man; [3] even the mysteries and elements of superstition that continued to haunt the private observances of town and countryside; finally, the burgeoning worship of the saints, the fragmentation or bureaucratization, if you will, of the essential purity and all-efficacy of the divine power. All this flows quite naturally from the Roman spirit and makes a profound impact upon the content and form of Christian literature. To its Roman antecedents the early church also owed its pervasive feeling for order and law; the hierarchically organized structure of its government; its sense of mission as lawgiver to the nations; its conviction of manifest destiny; and its presumption that the text of Scripture has a fuller and secret meaning.[4]

The authority of Sacred Scripture, moreover, is only partly the result of the dogma of divine revelation, for it proceeds from a way of seeing things that is congenial to the Roman mentality, that is, the absolute authority of the written word that has survived the centuries. An equal respect is accorded to Vergil and Plato and to whatever survives from antiquity, and this is a tendency that the Fathers and the early Middle Ages confirmed and carried several steps further.[5] This attitude was further developed by the cult of erudition rather than originality.

Yet this is not a surprising development before the advent of widespread literacy and before printing had robbed the word of much of its inherent mystique, a culture where *auctor* as a concept always has overtones of authority. Neither must we be surprised to note that, in keeping with the Roman mentality, there is always a strong interaction between form and content. These elements pass almost unconsciously into the Christian ambience and are subordinated to the Christian's sense of the otherworldly, which in itself accounts for the fact that Christianity did not subsume all these divergent strains with perfect harmony.

Tradition, one of the most cherished Roman traits, had certainly not been lost in the patristic era.[6] Men like Tertullian, Ambrose, Jerome, and Augustine were thoroughly in sympathy with the grandeur handed down authoritatively by Rome. This conservative tendency took the form of holding fast to a *depositum fidei,* revealed faith entrusted to the keeping of the Church by Christ himself. Much of the inherent content of this *depositum*—dogmas such as primacy, Incarnation, Trinity, predestination, grace—were slow to develop, in times free from persecution or as a reaction against the gropings of heresy.

Heresy is, of course, essentially a pejorative word, but here it is a concept that needs to be evaluated in the light of its own times. In these early centuries it is more properly understood as a tentative expression of Christian philosophy. It thus becomes one of the polarities of a Christian truth, at first uncritically believed by the simple and then upon reflection seen to contain some obvious inconsistencies. It provokes a reaction, and the resultant synthesis emerges as the authoritative statement of the Christian philosophy or, at a later date, as dogmatic truth. Heresy in these later years becomes heresy only after it has lost its debate with what emerges as orthodoxy. At first it appears to have an equal claim to win out as the truth. It is well to stress this point for the insight it provides into the Christian attitude.

Christian intolerance of pagan opinion is characteristic of a society that has either a conviction of the correctness of its official position or a sense of such imperative and categorical reaction against contamination from any source external to itself that not even the admittedly positive contributions of such an outside culture, not even those elements that would have been most advantageously included in the Christian synthesis, dare be tolerated.[7] This intransigent position had characterized the writings of those of the early Fathers who lacked the education to appreciate it, and in the fourth century this fear of subtle contamination was still very much in evidence. The resulting intolerance is certainly not humanistic, especially when the opposing views are founded upon a philosophy that is dictated by the highest traditions of classical culture, or when, as in the case of many of Jerome's adversaries, they are a corrective reaction against what is seen as an improper development in the Christian philosophy itself. This is not to say that heresy is good or Christian dogma bad, but that the tension between the two forces in the fourth century needs to be viewed in a more sympathetic light.

Faith and Revelation

The basic position of the Christian philosophy is generally characterized as faith, *fides,* a concept that has been subjected to considerable scrutiny and definition in the Christian theology. For present purposes, we need note only one point: the faith of the humanist should be in *humanitas,* as it was in classical times, whereas the Christian faith is faith in God or Christ.

Now, this distinction does not cut off the Christian philosophy from all claim to insight into, and expression of, true humanism. Faith can be (and early is) a powerful stimulus to philosophy, for it opens the way to the contemplation of elements in human nature that otherwise never would have been appreciated.[8] In the great Church Fathers one feels instinctively that this is the case. Yet here, too, Christian faith learned to focus more on the wonders of man's role in the world than to consider his eternal goals so transcendent an objective as to monopolize all his human energies.

The enthusiastic and inspired element of faith has always been part of the Christian tradition. Like inspiration, however, the element of faith soon loses much of its personal immediacy and becomes largely a preamble to acceptance of infallible truth. It was to some measure the failure, by the fourth century, of the Christian philosophy to provide adequate dialectic expression and foundation for the truths it proposed to the faithful that prompted it to have recourse simply to the "rule of faith," that is, the dogmatic assertion of a fact, and to revert to *mysterion*, that is, an article of faith believed to be true but still incapable of positive demonstration because of the weakness of human reason.

This is a position where Christianity had stood once before and to which it would again return. There was a more positive sense of *mysterion* as impetus to personal faith and commitment in the earlier years. The manifest errors of the second-century apologists and the positions taken by the third-century philosophers, fluctuating within the polarities of spirit-flesh and idealism-materialism, eventually give rise to the Christian solution of negative approaches: the Christian philosophy was content to demonstrate that truths were not inherently contradictory or repugnant to human reason.

Whether one chooses to see it as an advantage or hindrance in the long run, the fact that Christianity does claim to draw upon an absolute source of authority, and hence credibility, for its philosophy is certainly the most ponderable element of discontinuity with the past. The proud conviction of divine revelation, a deposit of truths that impinge upon the world of human experience from without and bear the clear stamp of credibility by virtue of their being vouched for by God himself, is a new and heady ingredient. It made the Christians an enthusiastic church of martyrs and evangelists. In time, however, it too came to function as material for the workings of the philosophic mind, once the passage of years had eliminated the need for compelling demonstration of the concept as a basis for the unfolding of the Christian philosophy. Yet even apart from the Christian's need to retain his early enthusiasm, the Incarnation made serious demands upon the philosophical acumen of early Christianity.

The duality of sources presents a real problem. True humanism, the purist might well argue, should be restricted to the use of purely natural resources. Although it was argued that the supernatural source of information could yield valuable insights into the human situation and destiny, eventually the formal differences between the two approaches betrayed the attempt at fusion.

Fundamentally, and in actual fact, the Fathers did not mean to urge too great a distinction between the realiability of those truths that came via divine revelation and those that came via the light of natural reason. There was, they presumed, a continuum in the economy of salvation that provided for the sure progression of what was known, of old, by light of human reason into what came ultimately from the same source, God, by a uniquely different and more credible way. More credible, that is, not in terms of its ultimate origins but in terms of its having taken a more direct route, less susceptible to the vagaries of human misinterpretation. By the fourth century, moreover, Christianity had already begun to develop its own ambience. So much theologizing had already been done upon the divinely guaranteed data of revelation that it was not always possible to distinguish between what was known originally via the unaided light of human reason and what had come through the medium of revelation. Much of what had indeed come from reason alone, but had taken a rather circuitous route, was made to flow instead from the sources of revelation as if it were a message straight from God, whereas in fact it had developed from the continuity with the classical past, not always classically remembered, and often in fact strangely distorted. Even where it was recognized and understood, the pagan classical heritage could not be simply taken over or even simply baptized. It would have seemed that the Incarnation had been to no avail if the humanistic philosophy inherent in Christianity had been too easily and too simply recast in classical terms. Even when, as in the case of Ambrose's *De Officiis*, the classical pagan philosophy does make its way into the patristic soul, the specifically Christian differences are generally stressed to the disadvantage of the pagan, which is to say that the cardinal virtues of prudence, justice, temperance, and fortitude are first of all baptized into their Christianized counterparts and then almost immediately relegated to a position of lesser importance than that enjoyed by the theological virtues of faith, hope, and charity. These virtues, in their turn, undergo a curious development, progressing from the virtues imposed by a sort of necessity upon the downtrodden classes who first embraced the Gospel to a position in which they are, so to speak, virtues only by analogy. It is the sheer gratuity of the Christian-infused virtues that is stressed. They come essentially as a free gift from God and are not the product of any human striving. Still, no purely human act is meritorious, in the supernatural order, without the foundation laid by these virtues in the soul of the elect.

The doctrine of grace, as it takes on more precise

form, lent further impetus to the development of an otherworldly orientation. It helped to set the unfortunate polarity of nature-grace, thereby asserting that nature is of itself evil and that its only salvation lies in its being elevated to the higher order of grace. This point of view tended to absolve the human agent of some human effort and further blunted his sensitivity to the humanistic culture. The search was now for the security of the supernatural and the comfort of dogma, in place of the challenge of using the world and living the Christian paradox by honoring the claims of both nature and grace. The rapid emergence of dogma from the *humanitas* of philosophy is regrettable, if only because dogma is of its very nature more intransigent and less open to religious inspiration, whereas a true Christian humanism needs to promote largely the opposite objectives.

What theology does in essence is to press for a science, that is, rigorous dogmatic theology. This involves an abuse of the language of Scripture, reducing the Bible's inspiration to the more sterile guarantee of inerrancy, and thus tending to cloud the appreciation of the Bible as literature. Words in theology must taken on technical force, and the expression of high religious enthusiasm hardens into a search for literal meaning so that the terms can function as the precise medium of revelation. Frequently this process involves reading something into the text. There are subtle changes in important words, where the meaning appears to be the same, in connotation, bearing, and intent, whereas in fact it has undergone considerable modification in order to function as the vehicle of scientific argument.

This process of development and adaptation is seen as a providential one, with God working through the very imperfections of his chosen human instruments. This conviction does much to explain why theology, in its search for precise demonstration of dogma, does not always hold fast to the obvious and literal meaning of words. Arguments frequently can be supported by allegory, adapted senses, typology, even by outright error in translation. From the humanistic point of view this is an abuse of language, and it invites a further abuse.

Gnosis

Side by side with the development of dogma we note the rise of that occultist tendency to find the Gospel still speaking its mysteries, no longer in terms of the original religious challenge and vision, or, again, in terms of what had formerly served as the raw material for dogmatic theology, but as an epiphenomenon, a growth upon the letter that would assure the occultist satisfaction of the need to be transcendentally reassured.[9]

Gnosis is a term applied to a group of self-styled elite within the Christian religion, although it had its pagan antecedents and counterparts. It has close ties with Neo-Platonism and the concept of knowledge through purification (the Essenes of the Dead Sea are a further analogue). As a doctrine it was gradually abandoned after the third century, when dogma had become more defined and there was less scope for writing one's own bill as a Christian. As an ascetic principle, characteristic of that group in every age to whom the Spirit really speaks, it is as abiding a factor within Christianity as is the Creed and the unshakable authority of the Roman Pontiff.

This urgency to exploit the letter of the text for other than its obvious meaning was largely the result of changes in the Christian structure itself. There had been considerable flux in the first centuries of Christian thinking, and Harnack is not far wrong in asserting that the

Church has done well to reread her past in order to discover a unified development, at least in retrospect, where there had been precious little of it in actual fact. But now in place of flux and enthusiasm and inspiration, we have the harder stuff of dogma. Revelation had closed with the death of Saint John the Apostle, and all new thinking had to make explicit that which was already implicit in the sources of revealed truth. This framework imposed upon the development of Christian philosophy proved to be a wonderful source of unity and coherence. But it also made it difficult to rediscover the faith and enthusiasm inherent in Christianity by the truly human sense, that is, by going back in time to encounter this new phenomenon in all its original force and coming to grips with its true religious message. Much of the early spirit had not been adapted and transformed, and there were other important objectives to be pursued in theology.

Still, this fascination with the letter pursues the letter in a peculiarly nonhumanistic manner and for nonhumanistic purposes. We should feel today that if the Gospel has a message for us it must be as a document of high religious fervor, in keeping with the proper human use of language. When this *sensus obvius* is forced into *terminus technicus* or a "fuller sense," other even less legitimate purposes are pursued. Then it is inerrancy that speaks, a preoccupation that is nonhumanistic simply because it is superhumanistic. And, as every true humanist might justly fear, the nonhumanistic rapidly develops into inhumanism, just as the superhumanistic will generally turn out to be antihumanism.

There is, moreover, a difference with respect to the methodology of ages past. The basic dilemma of human existence was not customarily solved in the classical pagan myths and their literary development in tragedy.

It was, rather, sympathetically stated, and always retained something of its inherent mystery. The dogmatic development of Christianity, on the other hand, embarked upon a somewhat different route. It gleaned elements of dialectic reasoning from the *mythos* of Scripture, through a process that does not always assure the survival of the religious inspiration of the sacred text, too often sacrificing enthusiasm for what proved to be merely logical afterthought or grammatical superstructure. This overrefinement resulted from confusing the literary genres of the sources and from reducing the utterances of the religious spirit to unencumbered statements of dogma. Christianity needed to be disabused of the notion that it could solve the fundamental problems of human existence other than in principle and for the few. The process was long and painful.

Classical humanism had, moreover, an aesthetic and anthropocentric view of man, whereas Christian humanism, even in its fullest flower, had a considerable mistrust of any real involvement with aesthetics as a primary ingredient of its world view. Aesthesis was too readily identified with decadence in the Roman culture of the early Christian centuries. This regrettable fact is, perhaps, one of the clearest marks of discontinuity between the Christian and the classical ideals; and it is owing, not to any shortcomings in the Christian Gospel, but largely to the degeneration of true classicism into the pagan culture encountered by Christianity.

The Christian ideal does suffer by comparison with the pagan classical ideal, in that it does not easily achieve either the balance or the awareness of human limitation—in a word, the thoroughgoing humanism we have come to associate with the full flower of the classical pagan ideal. It was a very long time before the Christian life fused with the pagan form to achieve a true appreciation of man's place in the universe, and even then this picture was quickly lost. Christianity is a ferment, and one hard to assimilate because it feeds upon, and thus destroys, much of what is really in its own best interests to preserve and develop. All of this simply illustrates the fact that theology and humanism are not universally compatible, and that certitude from God is too overpowering a credential.

Now, the element of religion as an ingredient of the humanistic philosophy might, as we have seen, be seriously challenged. The classical ideal must be seen as flowing from a consideration of human nature. Faith becomes compatible with human experience simply because the Christian does not always, in practice, reflect on the distinctions. In theory, however, there is always a potential problem: the individual will focus alternately upon one or the other polarity.

Otherworldly

The most serious shortcoming of Christian humanism proved to be the growing preoccupation with the otherworldly. The afterlife became a preponderant element of the Christian's striving. *Natalicia*, birthday, became in fact the day of birth into heaven, not into earth. This same tendency is evident in other words. The shift in meaning of *humanitas* has already been noted, but one might also note how meekness and *humilitas* became objects of human effort instead of qualities to be avoided; how self-denial became more essential a virtue than temperate enjoyment; and how the paradox was exploited that true life is seeming death. In a word, the chief theoretical claim of the Incarnation was to have produced the *novus Adam*, to have harmonized *Logos* and *homo*, the human and the divine in human destiny. Soon the divine emerges as the preponderant concern: it is no longer a question of how manlike God has become, but rather how godlike man must become.

In the fourth century this preoccupation with the otherworldly had more than theoretical and philosophical consequences. Christian religious enthusiasm had from the very beginning expressed itself in terms of extreme dedication to the ideals of the Gospel. Persecution and martyrdom, or imprisonment in the name of Christ, characterized the careers and ambitions of the Christians of the first centuries. The fourth century, however, introduced a new heroic ideal for the Christian who really meant to live up to his faith. With the cessation of persecution and the consequent removal of an ever-present threat to life and freedom of expression, the Christian seems to have turned to a new and self-imposed challenge to preserve and constantly renew on a personal level the imminent urgency of the Gospel imperatives. The tendency had already expressed itself in terms of the chiliast enthusiasm, which is to be found as early as Saint Paul, the conviction that the second coming of Christ was near at hand.[10] By the fourth century this hope for the imminent Parousia had dropped from focus, only to be replaced by a highly developed sense of *askesis*, not directed toward philosophical experience, but simply as a mark of the true Christian.

Askesis itself is not new. There had long been a doctrine of catharsis, a self-refinement for the contemplative soul, but the Gospel provided an added impetus.[11] Its overenthusiastic extension to the world at large involved painful adjustment. The controversies and tensions thus created will require some later discussion.

The Christian is, after all, a citizen of two worlds, a man of two cities, in the classical formulation of Augustine. His roots lie ultimately in both sources. On the one hand he has the mythology of the past with its human-

izing (rather than anthropomorphizing) creation of a
pantheon of deities who are really the larger editions of
man himself; on the other hand he has a heritage of
heaven after earth. The pagan religious ideal had sought
to focus attention upon the individual's fullest development of his inherent human potential. The Christian was
slow to appreciate or accept this essentially ennobling
view of human nature and to enlist it in the service of
his own *mythos*. His world view too soon became an
otherworld view. The Christian on the road toward
Christian humanism needed, despite his calling to an
afterlife, ideally, to make use of the world and even of
the lustful and rebellious flesh itself before he could
achieve his goal as Christian. He needed to be human
before he could be truly Christian, and to be a Christian
man before he could aspire to become a saint. For centuries this ideal was neither fully realized nor resolutely
pursued.

When the proper balance in objectives was finally
achieved, it came about, paradoxically enough, because
of a change in focus. Christianity began eventually to
function less as religious impulse than as atmosphere or
backdrop. Much of what the Christian religion appeared
to incorporate turned out, after the cooling effect of
three centuries, to be merely a trend name for things that
happened in a world become Christian. Much of what
savored of the Christian world view was a Christian
world view turned Establishment, with vested interests
of its own. As such, it was ripe for a total reassessment
of a heritage that it had failed to recognize in its infancy.
It required the slow gestation of centuries to give birth
to the new humanism as a proper harmony of the Christian philosophies of world and afterworld. The full
achievement of this happy coalescence was not simply
the product of the fourth Christian century; and one
might well criticize the fourth century for failing to

achieve what it was uniquely qualified to achieve, for having let slip an opportunity that was destined never again to appear, or at least not for many centuries.

The degree of Christian humanism achieved by the fourth century is still a true and genuine humanism. Our scholarly judgment tends to single out mostly its shortcomings if we fail to consider that Christianity was building upon the antique rather than the classical heritage of ages past. We are in a position today to realize the failings more acutely because we can compare the acme of classical pagan humanism with what in many respects is only the earliest stage of the Christian humanism that later flowered in the Renaissance. Although our judgment is thus, in many respects, better founded than the less critical awe displayed by the Middle Ages for Patristic humanism, we must not swing too enthusiastically to the opposite extreme.

Christianity and Classics

The first Christian centuries had been marked by two different and not always consistent attitudes toward the pagan classical heritage in its literary form. Strong and sympathetic support came from those of the Fathers who were educated in the rhetorical and literary tradition of antiquity, appreciated the possible continuity between Christianity and its classical antecedents, and recognized the need to use pagan philosophy as a tool in the evolution of the Christian view of the world. Many others, conversely were more aware of the failings of contemporary pagan classicism (while they were unable to recover the true classical humanism), of the need for a reaction against persecution, and of the precedence of otherworldly claims upon Christian allegiance.

The major representatives of these two opposing attitudes are too familiar to require any discussion here. One should, however, note that a balanced judgment on these matters is all but impossible. If the scholar searches, he can draw up a surprisingly full documentation for either position, often within the oeuvre of one and the same Father. Even those who most mistrusted pagan learning felt the need to draw upon its basic forms of expression.

There are a good many studies, general and specific, that explore the patristic relationship with the classics. Hagendahl, for example, has, most recently, compiled a listing of Saint Augustine's indebtedness to the pagan authors,[12] and the subject is amply treated in the indexes of every scholarly edition of the patristic writings. But merely listing and identifying the sources is not enough. The simple fact of quotation does not indicate the attitude with which the Fathers regarded their classical heritage. The fact that we call these works classics today does not mean that the Fathers looked upon them as classics in anything like the Renaissance or modern sense. That would have been a difficult perspective to achieve, particularly in the face of prejudices that all tended to a quite opposite evaluation. The involvement with pagan philosophy, to which infant Christianity turned for methodology and a frame of reference, was not really humanistic. What was needed was the conversion of a humanist or the thoroughgoing classical training of a sympathethically minded Christian.

The opposition to the classics that appears to some of the Fathers is characterized by mistrust and misinformation. Those Fathers who have any valid claim to represent the Christianized humanism of classical times stand at best several times removed from the true mentality of the works they meant to build upon. We must never overlook the havoc wrought by discontinuity in this respect. The reconstruction of the classical ideal, even where openly and enthusiastically attempted, was curiously incomplete: inadequate in principle, subjective, biased, it sought demonstration and proof for the validity of something characteristically Christian that was supposedly founded upon its antecedents in the classical past, whereas it was, in fact, quite different in identity and spirit.

This dual stream influenced the fourth century as well, where the issue was further complicated by the predominance of otherworldly orientations. But another factor that needs to be considered is the ad hoc and practical character of much patristic writing, which was thus often deprived of those classical humanistic ideals so essential to the literature of power as opposed to the literature of knowledge: the gratuitous development of an ideal theme as sufficient in itself to motivate and justify the artistic expression. We are dealing too much with the literature of knowledge or an attempted literature of power too hastily composed.[13]

The influence of noble pagan thought was obvious in every century, and particularly in the fourth. Early scholarship, aware of these trends, described the resultant product as pagan form and Christian content. Today we are more likely to recognize a higher degree of continuity within the content as well. There is thus a survival and contamination in genre as well as in the manner of expression.

Patristic Literature

The literary genres of early Christian writings have not received the same attention that has been accorded to biblical exegesis. The Roman had, after all, a sense of form unique in the history of literature: he knew what was the proper vehicle for history, epic, satire, love poetry, a letter of consolation, or a panegyric. His sense of form led him to realize his creative inspiration only within the framework of a well-established genre or style. Painstaking emulation of one's predecessors was considered grounds for praise and recognition; thus the Roman literary mentality was not prepared to accept novelty. Its peculiar literary genius was more sympathetic to a sense of developing tradition within the well-marked limits of a specific genre.

It would be strange indeed if the Roman Church Fathers did not exhibit a similar awareness. Augustine's *Confessions* are, seen in this continuity, a sort of meditative soliloquy. The *City of God,* which embodies the first attempt at a Christian philosophy of history, is, in other respects, a potpourri in the Roman tradition of the prose medley. Its historical and literary sources may or may not be manifold, but the style and form exhibit the later Latin preoccupation with anthologizing and excerpting of earlier authors. Jerome's *Letters* might have sprung from the pages of Quintilian as model developments of the stock rhetorical forms and styles: so much so, in fact, that scholars seriously doubt whether some of them were not written without any application to a real situation, as a *jeu d'esprit* on the part of that most classically learned of all the Christian authors, who languished for the rhetorical exercises of his youth. His *Treatise against Jovinian* is a fine specimen of the Roman style of *exempla,* anecdotes adduced as illustration of a thesis—which in Jerome's case is simply that women are no good. The fact that Jerome, in this context, appears to confuse illustration with proof is evidence, not of his having departed from the genre of *exempla,* but rather of the theological shallowness of many patristic polemics. The Scripture commentary develops after Origen on the lines of the standard *explication de texte*, such a natural if not always congenial instructional methodology that it would be strange indeed if any epoch in the history of education has ever been wholly without it. The sermon, or homily, also a written composition, has manifold antecedents: the philosophic essay, the diatribe, the rhetorical declamation, like which it often displays more brilliance than concern for evoking, in Bossuet's phrase, "the gift of tears"—that is, conviction and conversion in the listener.

There is growing awareness among the students of the Patristic Age of these continuities between Christian and pagan Roman literary endeavor. We are concerned here with the non-Christian character of much that looks like Christian writing, those elements of continuity with the Roman tradition that extend more to matters of detail and content.

Chief among these is the Roman development of the tradition of *topoi*, or literary commonplaces, stock themes that run throughout the history of literature. Unlike our modern age, antiquity attached no stigma to the employment of *topoi*. It was, in fact, a matter of pride to exploit them in novel ways. The literary history of individual commonplaces and their development well into the Middle Ages is a rewarding study.[14] In a more general way, an awareness of these tendencies must enhance the appreciation of any individual patristic author. We shall see that this is particularly true of Jerome, largely perhaps because of his excessive involvement with mere words.

Christian patristic scholarship on this subject has been curiously hampered by a naïve unwillingness to assume that the Fathers were actually using rhetorical and stylistic commonplaces, as if these were somehow at variance with truthfulness and, as such, outside the arsenal of patristic expression. When Prudentius says he "saw these very things himself," it was immediately believed that he had done so; when Jerome alludes to the vices of his earlier years, he is taken at face value. When the Christian writer belabors his unworthiness or his incapacity for artistic expression, it passes for genuine humility. When he asks God to aid his endeavors, it is made to sound like true prayer rather than a Christianization of the pagan invocation to the Muses.

Not only did the Fathers employ a considerable number of *topoi* that echo the Roman tradition; Christian literature itself soon evolved a well-stocked repertory of Christianized *topoi* of its own. This applies not only to the obvious substitution of Christian elements for pagan within the same context (like the invocation to God or the Saints instead of the Muses) or to areas where the words sound Christian to us because we are more familiar with them as classical commonplaces (for example, protestations of unworthiness—*humilitas*), but also to many stock themes that are presumed to be the proper expression of the sentiments of a good Christian. This makes for difficulties in interpretation and requires a balanced judgment in assessing the true bearing of a patristic expression. Much of the Christian disparagement of classical antiquity is not a matter of genuine conviction: it is conventional. Often, moreover, the very form of expression belies the content. One need only work his way through the first book of Augustine's *Confessions* to appreciate this striking divergence between content (disparagement of classical literature) and the vehicle of its expression, which is Roman and classical, and jubilantly so. There is a longstanding Roman tradition, of course, for precisely this convention: see, for example, Horace's disclaimers to epic expertise in

Scriberis Vario (*Odes* 1.6), or in the opening lines of
Satires 2.1.

In a conservatively oriented and derivative literature
such as the Latin patristic writings, content is often
largely determined by borrowed forms. Continuity in
traditional genres and individual commonplace made
it a point of honor to emulate, within a traditional
framework, the established works of those who were
acknowledged masters in that field. The older catch-
phrase "pagan form and Christian content" is still partially correct, because the Christian author had a different message from that of pagan literature; but the form,
too, must be seen as exerting a kind of mortmain upon
the content, not only in its phrasing, but often in essential elements of its point of view.

The very fact that patristic literature looked to earlier
classical forms as a model and was aware of some continuity already precludes, at least in part, the full accomplishment of one cherished ideal of the true humanist. The patristic writer might indeed claim to be enlisting
the past as the model for the present; but his horizons
had grown too narrow. Continuity was largely restricted
to form and the influences of form upon content. The true
dimensions of the classical vision, which we might hope
the patristic age could have recaptured, always hover
beyond its grasp.

Christianity and Latin

The Latin literary language, as we have seen, is a
facile tool for the humanist, the vehicle for the expression of Roman *humanitas* and fashioned for this purpose. As the form determining the totality of structure
and vision within pagan classicism, it soon dissipated;
but many elements survived, reinforced by the rhetorical

bent of later education and its preoccupation with gathering *bons mots* from the past. These elments provided rich material for the Christian who was eager to apply even the most rudimentary humanism in language to the expression of his Christian faith.

Unfortunately, it is not always the best elements that survived. One of the most obvious of the inherited techniques is antithesis; inherent in any language, it is a more-developed stylistic element in the flexible word order of the Latin sentence. Latin thus fitted in providentially well with Christian paradoxes and polarities, to whose expression it lent such a ready support that the results, in the hands of men who lacked the fullness of classical form and harmony, were an exaggerated attention to elaborate antithesis as a normal pattern for developing their thought. Such a stylistic imbalance soon reduced the impact of the paradoxical. Like much of the earlier pagan conceits of style, the striking became commonplace.

In terms of the Christian Gospel itself, there was a more serious consequence: an overemphasis on the isolation, and eventually the mutual exclusivity, of the two terms in the polarities of earth-heaven and flesh-spirit, rather than the promotion of their happy coalescence as contributing elements to one harmonious view of man in God's world. This was, after all, the greatest potential contribution of the Incarnation, the theoretical fusion of Alpha and Omega. It would be naïve to blame the Latin language for this failure of the Christian potential; yet, in the developing Christian literature the ready use of these stylistic elements within the Latin tradition accentuated the process.

In this connection we must mention the phenomenon of vocabulary shift, a subtle tendency that may escape the notice of even the observant student of comparative cultures and institutions—largely by reasons of its slowness and of the easily overlooked difficulty of mastering any idiom other than one's native tongue. One recognizable process is that by which originally undifferentiated words assume a new range of technical meaning. Examples abound in the Christianized glossary: presbyter, grace, baptize, martyr, pope—all become realities of a new order. Jerome contributed to the formation of more than 350 words; Lactantius and Tertullian provided many more. Many new words were required, and there were many new sources on which to draw: the Hebrew Old Testament, the Greek Koine, the specialized vocabulary of the New Testament. There were also many new concepts that still developed within the protective shell of the older words. *Humilitas*, for example, has already been discussed, as has *humanitas*. The nomenclature of the virtues might remain externally the same, but Christian self-control or continence does not correspond exactly with the pagan concept of an inner harmony with the ideal.

A more subtle shift lies in the connotative overtones that develop for many words, eventually forming an obstacle against the recovery of classical humanism and its outlook. These words are to be found everywhere in the Christian writings: *martyr, natura, saeculum, anima, mors, castitas, virgo*. It is only the connotative overtones that change, and thus the bridge with the antique past appears to be continuous, whereas it is in fact a ghost over broken ruins. The Christian conception of the otherworld is largely responsible for this shift, and it is a natural phenomenon and thus to be anticipated. Failure to recognize these facts can weaken the reliability of later judgment on the accomplishments, purposes, and *humanitas* of the patristic era.

Jerome

Christianity had reached this stage in realizing its potential as a humanistic culture by the fourth century. With the cessation of persecution, Christian thinkers were in a position to address themselves to problems other than those of survival. The fourth century is also characterized by a significant measure of discontinuity with the classical past, as we have seen, so that any real sense of appreciation for that era was not largely a matter of rediscovery. It was a time when champions were needed, men whose grasp of Christianity was sympathetic to humanism, who were acquainted with the classical heritage and able to understand with much the same eyes and ears as did the audience for which the mature products of classicism were first enunciated.

Now there were, in fact, men of this caliber in the fourth century in the Latin West. Traditionally we number Augustine, Ambrose, Lactantius, and Jerome among the greatest of the Western Church Fathers. Here we shall consider only one individual Christian humanist who, among fourth-century Christian writers, far outranks all others in his grasp of Roman and Greek antiquities. His peculiar frame of mind made him particularly conscious of his debt to classical culture yet aware of those specifically Christian elements that needed to be safeguarded in any confrontation with the heritage of ages past. This man is Saint Jerome.

Jerome has been presented as a man whose avowed mission it was to fuse all the best elements of both his worlds into the synthesis of Christian humanism.[15] This traditional evaluation bears some sympathetic review. It is of course to be expected that his humanism would necessarily labor under the disadvantages of his time, when pagan humanism was neither well recalled nor yet fully rediscovered in a Christian setting, and the Christian element itself had begun to suffer from improper definition of its ideal, citizenship in two worlds.

Jerome's reputation is, moreover, essentially a product of the Middle Ages, whose judgment on the Church Fathers we have largely inherited and long tended simply to preserve. The medieval judgment on Jerome was based on much imprecise information and colored by the medieval community of purpose with the objectives of Jerome's own career. We need to reexamine particularly those areas in which Jerome was most highly honored and esteemed: his erudition, his Vulgate translation of Scripture, his commentaries, his skill in using words, and his orthodox championing of the cause of asceticism.

The shortcomings of erudition as a claim to literary fame could hardly be appreciated in an era like the Middle Ages, which were themselves more given over to erudition than to creative originality. In their way, they overvalued Jerome's actual acquaintance with the classical past. The unquestioned accomplishment of the Vulgate translation could too easily obscure the equally unquestioned weakness of much of Jerome's commentary and the tendentious intrusion of Jerome's own personal thinking into what he sets forth as the fuller meaning of the sacred text. The evaluation is, finally, largely a product of monkish ideals. Only the clergy were in a position to read and understand much of his work, and their enthusiastic appreciation of, and community with, his objectives have endowed his memory with a position of precedence, from which any subsequent evaluation has first of all to dislodge him before it can arrive at an objective point of view. In spite of detailed modern study of many of the points upon which Jerome's reputation rests, the essentials of the medieval attitude have not been really touched, and scholars have not yet embarked upon a full-scale reevaluation. The attitudes inherited from the Middle Ages, though ultimately based on a set of judgments no longer entirely supportable, have nonetheless influenced our contemporary attitudes. When the Renaissance took up the subject of Saint Jerome, it had already inherited the traditional judgment; Renaissance writers took delight in the words Jerome had bequeathed them and were not concerned to discover how superficial much of his familiarity with the classical ideals might be. They were concerned with the excitement of rediscovery of what they presumed him to have known, and they were not put off by the strange bias of much of what passes for orthodox Christianity in Jerome.

One curious and significant fact soon begins to emerge. The student of Jerome who takes pains to rediscover the venerable doctor in the light of the fourth century inevitably becomes aware of his many shortcomings. Because Jerome was no proponent of the golden mean, his strong points each developed a contrary failing. The very elements in his career and makeup that enabled him to see the challenge and urgency of his ultimate objectives were precisely what hindered him from bringing his work to a successful conclusion. This statement is more far-reaching in application than might appear. It affects not only such obvious considerations as tendentious scriptural exegesis and overenthusiastic spiritual advice, but also his very methodology and direction. In this connection there are many individual points to be briefly considered.

Erudition and Rhetoric

Jerome's manifest acquaintance with, and appreciation for, Roman literature and philosophy would appear to be an obvious claim to humanism. His erudition was the product of the best schooling available in his day (Donatus and Victorinus) and of an intense personal involvement with the literature and language of classical Latinity. But the true dimensions of this involvement need some sober appraisal and study. His indebtedness to earlier authors frequently goes beyond the relationship of verbatim and acknowledged quotation. Whole sections are lifted from Cyprian, Tertullian, Theophrastus, Seneca; and there are constant briefer allusions, reminiscences, verbal plays, and echoes. His first book against Jovinian, for example, contains pages of this type of reference, a vast display of erudition if perhaps an unconvincing argument.

Since A. Lübeck first delved into the question of what pagan authors were known to Jerome,[16] succeeding generations of scholars have discovered more and more authors, pagan and Christian, Latin and Greek, that "Jerome knew." What has been generally ignored is the derivative character of much of Jerome's acquaintance. He had read some of these authors, not in the original text, but in essays and anthologies. Latin literature had, since the time of Cicero, delighted in series of *exempla*, pointed anecdotes or quotations designed to illustrate a theme. The related genre of the prose medley, originally a forerunner of the classical Latin *satura*, grew in vogue with the developing appetite for secondary literature that marks the epitomes so popular in the decline of Silver Latinity. Jerome is here largely a child of his times. The history of this later literature is filled with the names of epitomizers of major literary works of the past, minor compendia and manuals, as well as collections of curious anecdotes and antiquarian lore like the *Attic Nights*. Although much of this has come down to us, much more has mercifully been lost; and most of what we have now recovered of classical antiquity came into the hands of Jerome, and later of the Middle Ages, only in pericope. From another point of view, it is quite in keeping with the established Roman tradition to entertain this richness of quotation in one's literary work, in the expectation that the subtlety and brilliance of the allusion will be recognized and appreciated by the equally erudite reader. The question in Jerome's case is rather how well he actually knew the various authors from whom he quotes.

The question is further complicated by Jerome's less than candid manner of quotation. He appears to have made some deliberate effort to conceal the immediate sources from which he gathered material with which to grace his *exempla*. Jerome really appears to be quoting Seneca, Theophrastus, and others, in a rather loose form of reference, giving the impression that he has read them all at length.[17]

One is forced to admit that this type of literature is not in the very best interests of the humanist tradition because it is not truly involved with classical ideals and models either in content or in form, that is, in the ideal of balance, nobility of expression, and aesthetic harmony. It is, rather, a curious, anthologizing, and even anecdotal, preoccupation with the trivia of classicism, an involvement with a footnote literature that can easily preclude any higher sense of appreciation. What we encounter here, in a word, is discontinuity with the spirit and continuity only with the formal ornaments of classical humanistic literature and spirit.

Further disadvantages of such erudition are its penchant for verbal association rather than sense and meaning, and, at least in the case of Jerome, a well-indulged propensity to quotation. None of all this was known to the Middle Ages, who supposed instead that Jerome had mastered his sources by exhaustive and critical study. Had they recognized or suspected the truth of the matter, they might indeed have accused Jerome of a lack of candor. However, they would never have suspected, or have been willing to admit, a fact so out of harmony with the objectives of their own humanizing scholarship and reverential attention to the literature of the past.

Jerome was the product of an educational system that was hampered by serious defects. Rhetoric, with all its artificiality and divorced from any practical application to the political and social issues of the day, was the guiding light of Roman education in postclassical times. The rhetorical formation of Jerome's expression is evident: he is familiar with the precepts that prescribe the form and content of all the genres of declamation and composition. In fact, he quotes the masters of rhetoric with ease and launches upon an impressive defense of the polemical style of writing.[18]

One can indeed note some shift away from the exuberant display of rhetorical flourish that marks the *juvenalia,* the earliest letters, when, pining for an audience for his declamatory exercises, he appears simply to have written them out. The inherent artificiality of this style has prompted some question as to the genuineness of, for example, Letter 117, a *consolatio* along classical lines. Jerome apparently had more stylistic form letters and prescribed niceties of expression in his stockpile than the relatively circumscribed limits of his personal experience gave him opportunity to indulge without some play of imagination.

Certainly this rhetorical style was congenial to the development of the humanistic spirit, for an orator, Cicero himself, was the fountainhead of all Roman Latin humanistic expression. One of the truest marks of humanism, it has been pointed out, is the ability to harmonize the content of the thought expressed with the balance and nobility of its verbal expression. Rhetoric, when lacking in depth, becomes mechanical and displaces the critical sense; brilliance for its own sake is seldom refreshing for very long, and constant display is tiresome. Jerome, unfortunately, cannot pass by a single opportunity to play the rhetor.

On his subject, the Middle Ages and the Renaissance humanists might truly look to Jerome as an original and brilliant wielder of language. Having an incomplete picture of Jerome's debt to the classical tradition, and the long history of ready-made *bons mots* upon which he could draw, they were more inclined to regard his brilliance as original. They might have felt cheated to have discovered shortcomings in the master's creative genius.

Satire

In a recent book on Jerome as a satirist,[19] David S. Wiesen concludes that much of Jerome's polemic is simply that pleasurable and genial overstatement of one's point, which we commonly associate with the mainstream of Roman satire. Jerome himself appears to have intended this continuity with his Roman exempla.[20] One of the most typical characteristics of Roman satire is illustration by example: in order to understand all of the references to people and places, the student needs to master a whole index of proper names and references drawn from the personal or literary experience of the satirist and identified by centuries of painstaking scholarship. The impact of innuendo is lost unless the richness of all these allusions can be recaptured. Acting on the presumption that reference of this kind ought to proceed from personal experience, one might be inclined to criticize Jerome's lack of originality, in that his is purely imitative satire: there are few proper names that are the product of his own experience, and there is little personal observation, simply the most generic statements, about wine, women, merrymaking, the faults of some of the secular clergy, or vilification of his opponents in set formulas. Jerome would thus appear not to be a satirist in the Roman style.

Such an evaluation, however, fails to take into account some important facts. Jerome was justified in claiming spiritual kinship with the Roman satiric tradition in prose or verse. The mordant character of Roman satire is often dependent upon the careful manipulation of words. This careful attention to language precludes to some extent *autopsia*, that is, personal observation of the subject matter that is being satirized; *animus*, a strong held personal attitude against the objects of one's attack (like Juvenal's *indignatio*); and finally, even elaboration of the terms and *topoi* employed in the satire. The objective of the satirist is—at least, in part—to emulate his predecessor in the refined expression of commonplaces while making some personal contribution to the genre of satire.

Jerome, too, achieves this objective, though with lesser invention and a rather heavier hand. It is in this sense that he is most truly a satirist, not a man possessed by *indignatio* that simply swells into spontaneous vilification or the righteous wrath of God's holy ones. There must always be something of this lack of immediacy in Roman satire, with final composition several times removed from inspiration. One cannot sustain animus throughout the time it takes to write cleverly; although the objects of satire remain and the purpose may still wax strong, there is more scope for verbal display than for violent feeling.

We have seen that Jerome is not unsympathetic to

the Roman tradition of erudite quotation. Even when he is simply cataloging *exempla* from antiquity, Jerome could well count upon his readers' recognizing his sources and looking upon his use of them as stylistic embellishment and as evidence of his scholarly authority. The extensive use of quotation is indeed a hallmark of the satiric tradition and reaches its climax in Juvenal.

Jerome's satire in the fourth century, however, suffers from a certain discontinuity with classical satire. What survives of the Roman tradition are largely the lesser ingredients of satire: topicality, quotation, the borrowed phrase. The larger framework had already dissipated, and together with it much of the careful discipline and skill of composition. There has been relatively little discussion as to whether Jerome expected or wanted his readers to recognize his sources. If this was his desire, it would be an example of continuity with other satirists—Juvenal, for example, and Horace—and of the anthologizing tendencies of later Latin literature in general. But, as we have seen, though Jerome makes a conscious effort to parade his "bookshelf" of classical authors, he conceals its ultimate sources, which one must suspect are largely secondary —in Jerome's case, the lost misogynistic treatises of Porphyry and Seneca.

Jerome's position in the history of misogynistic literature is well established. Not only does he sum up the combined *topoi* from antiquity, but he also stands as the fountainhead from which much of the antifeminism of the Middle Ages flows. Misogyny, like satire, is neither particularly Christian nor humanistic in spirit, although it antedates (and may well survive) both Christianity and humanism. Historically it forms an understandable continuity within both traditions. The Roman church, like the society of the antique and classical past, was male-dominated. The Old Testament is male-oriented, as was the ancient Near Eastern culture upon which it drew. The fourth century had learned to view woman as something more than a ready target for satire. Woman presented an occasion for temptation and sin, which, in this context, is equated with unchastity. The pairing of this vice and the repertory of ancient antifeminist bromides is a powerful combination, particularly in the hands of a man who has a way with words and an ax to grind. Thus the bearing and the content of commonplace witticisms at the expense of womankind were altered. Jerome is further concerned with promoting the monastic vocation, and he himself shows a serious psychological eccentricity.

The curious taste of many of Jerome's examples and allusions is another case in point here.[21] In itself, there is nothing especially humanistic about scurrility, for it is a violation of that balance between nobility of thought and its harmonious verbal expression. There has always existed, however, a literary convention of scurrility,[22] with well-defined rules for its use. In Roman satire, point and spirit are gained by sophisticated language (like the educatedly ribald limerick), a mock-heroic quality that exploits the disproportion between the area of human experience being described and the vehicle of its description.[23] Jerome's style often goes beyond these nice limits.

There is, finally, a certain shock value in the use of less than perfectly decorous vocabulary and diction.[24] In Jerome's case one cannot always know what consideration have determined the tone and taste of his writing, but there is evidence to lead one to conclude that it is not always sophistication. Fundamentally it is not the highest classical tradition: the subject matter is allowed to outweigh care and attention to expression.

Language and Style

One point that emerges from an examination of the various genres and styles of composition that Jerome employs is his mastery and variety in mode and level of expression. This is in keeping with classical humanism: rhetorical propriety decrees that there be both a style and a level of diction for every occasion, and this is to be scrupulously observed, even in the breach, as, for example, in the case of mock epic.

In the exegetical works and commentaries Jerome is objective and sober, granted the prejudice of the Christian exegete for the fuller sense and typologies. It is only in his letters that he indulges in the rhetorical flourishes that later seem to have been corrected or restrained by maturity. The *Lives of the Desert Fathers* are jewels of careful composition, and the polemics range between the descriptive style of satire (that is, careful attention to words and diction in the sophisticated reviling of his adversaries) and the outpouring of ill humor against his opponents. In his use of the other genres he has some claim to classical humanism, but his polemical style argues a lack of true humanistic insight: Jerome reneges on the effort to couch his thought in the appropriate form and bring it to the proper level of elegance.

We may profitably examine Jerome's unquestioned way with words. He is first of all as translator, involved with the precise range of meaning in rendering the original Greek and Hebrew texts into Latin. Ancient translation in itself is not the finely accomplished rendering of sense for sense and poetry for poetry that we are accustomed to expect today, and, in the case of the Bible, there are other considerations as well. The force, sometimes the very presence, of idiom is often overlooked because of the conviction, already gaining in popularity during the lifetime of Jerome, that inspiration is inherent in the words themselves and not just in the message or the meaning. This conviction, and the understandable effort to perpetuate the message, results in a tendency to concentrate on the rephrasing of the original text in a one-for-one relationship, reproducing the words rather than the meaning, so that any deeper message, latent in the word but not clear to Christian thinking at that time, would not be lost for the contemplation of later ages.

Psalm 121 will serve as an example. The Vulgate translation contains the cryptic (and literal) rendition *Jerusalem quae aedificatur ut civitas, cuius participatio eius in idipsum.* The more recent Latin translation reads *in se compacta tota.* What is missed here is the force of an expression like the Greek εἰς τὸ αὐτό or ἐπὶ τὸ αὐτό, "together." In 1 Cor. 7 : 5 this same failure to recognize the idiom gives the reading *et iterum revertimini in idipsum*, which is then made to take on the sinister implication that the Apostle "blushes to refer to the sex act by name," using the phrase *id ipsum* as a substitute.[25]

Despite many errors, Jerome should be criticized only in the light of the better control enjoyed by modern scholars over the real meaning of words in ancient languages and of higher modern standards in the art of translation. The Vulgate is universally acknowledged as a supreme accomplishment, a brilliant wedding of reverential and elevated style with vocabulary and locution accessible to the common Christian and achieving the dignity and the immediacy proper to the sacred text. Further, the Vulgate, canonized in its turn, enjoys the same textual inviolability as did the original; profound theological argument has always exhibited a retrograde tendency to revolve about the word and letter rather than the underlying message and spirit of the sacred text.

The precise range of meaning, however, even in the translation of Scripture, is not what should always be most characteristic of the humanist's concerns. It is more the province of the theologian, a role Jerome was little qualified to assume. What the true humanist, in the fourth century, ought to have recognized was that considerable development had occurred and was still occurring in the very words he used. This is to be noted not only in Scripture, but in every area of the new Christian vocabulary.

Although the detailed methodology for the study of comparative vocabulary and connotative uses of words is not yet complete, many examples can still be adduced. A number of these words have already been pointed out. Perhaps the most obvious instance of Jerome's tendency to equate the connotative values of the Christianized vocabulary with the less differentiated usage of the same words in earlier authors is at the end of his first book *Against Jovinian*, where the word *virgo*, in its fullest Christian connotation—that is, a woman who has dedicated herself to Christ in perpetual chastity—is taken as a key word for stringing together a long list of *virgines Romanae et Graecae* who are held up as models for the Christian world and proof of the fact that virginity has ever been held in highest repute. As we shall later discover, the word *virgo* was dear to Jerome for other reasons as well.

Analysis of Latin word order in the writings of a particular author, a study developed by Marouzeau,[26] has two specific purposes: first, to determine how naturally the author writes Latin or to what era of Latinity his style must be assimilated; second, to determine how far he exploits the potential of Latin to express subtle nuance by shifts in word position. The verb in the Latin sentence, for example, depending upon its position as initial, medial, or final, can assume fine overtones of meaning; and the adjective, to achieve contrast or in order to invest a word with new force, can, for example, precede rather than follow its noun or even be separated from it by a brief disjunctive element. Similar observations hold true for the other parts of speech, and these elements all lend themselves to statistical analysis. Some work has been done along these lines with the text of Saint Jerome.[27]

Jerome's style, like that of many of his contemporaries, leans heavily toward the nonperiodic Senecan prose style. It is characterized primarily by a less involved syntax, shorter sentence patterns, and rhetorical display. The increased parataxis allows greater concentration on the potential for striking expression and clever nuance inherent in the nominal cluster (the noun and its adjectives or genitives) and the meaningful positioning of the verb.[28] This tendency has reasonably been called baroque, in that the style appears to set higher value upon ornamentation and detail than it does upon the classical ideal of total form. Scholars have seen these developments as a deviation, a losing sight of the true classical spirit. But it is also, and equally important for our study here, a ready technique for developing the Christian paradox. As such, it was popular long before the time of Jerome—so much so, it has been observed, that the paradox as a Christian insight into reality had lost a good measure of the force of the paradoxical and had become something of Christian commonplace. Jerome seldom misses an opportunity to exploit the emphasis or effect that can be achieved by variation in the position of words within their proper syntactic group. This tendency is observable to different degrees in the various genres of composition, but it is always in evidence.

There is, moreover, evidence that Jerome had succumbed to the temptation (or perhaps had fallen victim to the process) that seizes upon the humanist whose concern with capturing a culture not entirely contemporary in spirit to his own experience forces him to cast the substance of his thinking in the mold of a more antique expression. The antique language, in its terms and concepts and in its patterns of expression, exercises a sort of mortmain upon the content of what is said. This is particularly true of Latin, where the development of an adequately abstract and plastic medium for the expression of the classical ideal of the Golden Age is intimately interwoven with the very essence of that ideal itself. Form and content are thus so interdependent that the vitality of the one cannot (or at least does not, historically) really survive the decline and eclipse of the other.

If a modern scholar sets himself to compose in Latin, and really enters deeply into the spirit of the language, it is truer to say that Latin is writing through him rather than that he is writing Latin. There is evidence that this is already the case in the relationship between the fourth century and the classical past. A warm familiarity with the literary productivity of classicism is always a prime ingredient of the humanistic attitude, even if the quotation and imitation are more a superficial *jeu d'esprit* than a true allegiance to the ideal of the earlier humanism. In the case of Jerome there are many other factors to substantiate and reinforce this argument: his love of classical rhetoric, his involvement with a

purely verbal level of experience, his preoccupation
with words and meanings, his ready grasp of the actual
patterns of writing and *bon mots* from the past.

Scripture

The patristic usage of Scripture reached a climax
in Saint Jerome. One drawback to his undeniable accomplishments in this field was his extreme overfa-
miliarity with the sacred page. He knew it so well that
willy-nilly the quotations flood his mind. The famous
Letter 22, for example, might be studied as a classic
example of the cento form, a composition made up in
part of sheer scriptural quotation, not all of it apropos,
and loosely stitched together into a patchwork. He
personalizes and allegorizes Scripture and frequently
quotes or alludes with such passing brevity that a series
of determined editors have still not run down every
reference. The principle of organization is frequently
mere verbal association, facile but not always really
accurate. This is in keeping with the inherited literary
tradition: it functions as a sort of extension of the
"Great Books" prescribed for the educated man and
harmonizes well with the classical practice of learned
quotation. By the fourth century firsthand acquaintance
with Scripture gives rise to a body of Christian literature, and familiarity with its less widely known passages is the proud mark of the Christian scholar and
man of culture.

We have seen, however, that by the fourth century
Scripture was also becoming source material for theology. Hence, confusion arises as to the precise frame of
reference in which a given quotation is to be understood,
whether as learned display or as an attempt to demonstrate the infallible truth of a statement in a theological

context. This applies especially to the polemical use of Scripture, where context and purpose call for dogmatic proof based on the sacred text, but the style invites learned display in quotation and allusion. Whereas the commentary becomes the technical tool and repository of theology, and the homily applies Scripture for practical ends, the polemical usage of Scripture is often an excursus into a different realm, with little pretense to serious scholarship. The polemical application of Scripture in the Fathers is a subject that has received scanty attention. It is, however, especially in Jerome, a curious mixture whose basic elements can be at least briefly illustrated.

An interesting example is the tendentious equation of the force of an expression used in one context with its quite different application in a different setting. In *AJ* 1.7d Jerome quotes the Apostle's advice, "Do not deprive each other except perhaps by consent for a time, that you may give yourselves to prayer" (1 Cor. 7 : 5), in order to demonstrate that sex in marriage and Christian prayer cannot possibly coexist. He then points out that Paul also bids us to "pray always" (1 Thess. 5 : 17), and concludes that we are thus never "to be subject to the service of wedlock, for everytime I render my wife her due I cannot pray."

A scriptural expression is often pressed to yield a meaning it was not intended to bear in the original text. In commenting on the force of God's command to the first parents, "Increase and multiply and fill the earth," Jerome points out that this does not apply to Christians, whose "citizenship is in heaven" (*AJ* 1.16). This exploitation of a secondary word can be carried further, as in Letter 22.10, where Adam's original sin is described as being motivated by gluttony because it involved eating. Again, drawing upon his expertise in language and skill in translation, Jerome embarks upon learned if tendentious interpretations of such key words as *almah* in the Hebrew text of Isa. 7 : 14, defending and further restricting the bearing of the prophecy of the virgin birth.[29] He insists upon "chastity" as the proper rendering of *sophrosyne*, rather than "prudence," and coins a neologism *castificat*, "chastifies," in place of the more common reading "sanctifies" in *AJ* 1.27, 37. Jerome occasionally appears to miss the basic idiom, as we have already seen: εἰς or ἐπὶ τὸ αὐτό in 1 Cor. 7 : 5, for example. In this connection, however, Jerome can always fall back upon the fuller sense, the wealth of hidden meaning with which God has filled his sacred text. This, in turn, leads to further extensions of the literal meaning. There is allegorization, sometimes quite extended, and typology in the treatment of the deaths of Moses and Joshua in *AJ* 1.2 ff. There is mystical interpretation of proper names, of Rome at the end of the *Treatise against Jovinian*, or, more pointedly, of Lebanon (whiteness—of purity), of Sanir, of Hermon (which is said to mean "consecration"—of a virgin), *AJ* 1.30.

Jerome often indulges in numerology to support interpretation. The number *two* (the number of the sex act) is not a good number because in the Hebrew text of Genesis, God is not recorded as having seen that the work of the second day was good, though he finds the work of the other days good in Genesis 1 (*AJ* 1.16).[30] The Parable of the Sower furnishes ammunition in this same context: the 30, 60, and 100 that describe the yield refer to three ascending grades of virginity.[31]

In establishing a framework for his interpretation, Jerome is willing to support either of two opposing positions. If an Old Testament example corroborates his argument, he asserts the radical continuity of Old and New Testament revelation. If it contradicts his position, he then argues for the lack of continuity and emphasizes the newness of the Gospel mandate. The same ambivalence is noted in references to pagan examples. If the pagan model reinforces his point, then "Christians ought at least to equal the accomplishments of noble pagans"; but if the pagan is opposed to the Christian, it is divested of all authority as being without the tradition of the Christian revelation.

Jerome can also read between the lines of Scripture. In 1 Pet. 3 : 7, husbands are instructed to live with their wives *iuxta scientiam,* or *secundum scientiam,* and to "pay honor to the woman as the weaker vessel." This eventually is forced to mean that perfect chastity in wedlock is what the Apostle means to prescribe for Christians (*AJ* 1.7e).

In addition to adopting an intransigent interpretation of the Apostle's words about marriage and to developing his argument by an overly rigorous logic (*AJ* 1.7–9), Jerome also determines that there is a difference between what the Apostle desires Christians to do and what he only concedes to them in view of more serious possible evils (*AJ* 1.8). He also develops an argument based on noblesse oblige: the Christian cannot rest content with the imperfect moral obligations enunciated by the Old Testament (*AJ* 1.24a). Drawing upon superior familiarity with the sacred page, Jerome can easily outmaneuver the opponent who dares to close with him. Where Jovinian had appealed to Solomon as support for his argument in favor of a like reward in heaven for both the virgin and the married, Jerome takes up the same figure of Solomon as a man of considerable marital experience who had spoken strongly against the advisability of taking a wife (*AJ* 1.28a). Again, against the interpretation of the story of the wedding at Cana (John 2 : 1–9) that argues Christ's willingness to accept marriage as a way of life, Jerome counters that by going to a wedding party only once, Christ has instructed us to marry no more than once (*AJ* 1.46).

Now, much of the above might suggest the conclusion that Jerome is involved in demonstrable error in the polemical application of Scripture. There is one other facet of the patristic use of the Bible, however, that still needs to be considered. All the specific types and instances of quotation considered above—and they are no more than representative of a much larger selection—can serve primarily not so much to demonstrate as to reinforce the writer's sense of the unity of his source and to reestablish a living contact with the authority for, and inspiration of, his Christian theology and religion. This reassuring sense of unity derives from the fact that both authority and inspiration come via the same medium, and a subtle reinforcement of the basic position is achieved by reflecting, in an aside at times, how a given quotation corroborates the central truths under discussion. This methodology centers the writer's subject matter within a setting of homogeneous doctrine, all of whose elements illustrate at least the general background upon which the exegete bases his argument. They may also serve to test the validity of one element by establishing the harmony with which it adapts to all the other elements of the Christian religion. This process need not always involve the most logical interpretation of the texts; often there are applications and interpretations that derive allegory, interpretation of names, numerology, typology, and a "fuller sense."

The quotation, then, is meant, not as a full and proper demonstration, but as a reflection upon how harmoniously the whole edifice of Christian awareness fits together, and as an inspirational renewal of the sense of purpose and dignity of the Christian vocation that is dictating the objectives of the polemical writing. The liturgical setting of many of these texts further enhances the immediacy and effectiveness of the process. The purpose and methodology of the early Christian liturgy and homily involve constant and pointed repetition, in mythic form, of the basic truths of the faith, such that their very familiarity and the noble grandeur of their liturgical expression [32] (and here the Roman *gravitas* stands out to fullest advantage, as does the Roman's involvement with exact expression of dogmatic truth) become a powerful tool for understanding the fundamentals of the Christian religion. If understanding is humanly impossible, these texts serve to fix the correct terms of the dogmatic statement of the mysteries and find practical application in motivating a life of special dedication. Scripture and the catechism of Christian doctrine take on a particularly compelling tone when the words are encountered in a sacral and liturgical context. This consideration, incidentally, explains why the quotation often runs far beyond the point where it properly applies to the argument and thus invites a sort of meditative vagary that, in its way, accomplishes the very same objectives.

Even apart from this liturgical encounter, private reading of Scripture nourished the piety and conviction of these men, and the word of the Bible was always close at hand when they came to pondering the basic realities of Christian life. The patristic attitude toward Scripture is thus perhaps best described as omnidirectional, and the primary concern for one of the various possible applications of the sacred text must never be taken to exclude the simultaneous application of others as well.

There is, in Jerome's case, the further element of

authority as an interpreter of the sacred word. The translator has a position of special privilege as interpreter of what he has translated, especially if he has in his youth copied and translated the commentaries of the mighty Origen and other learned men, and thus can support his own views and opinions with copious authority. Jerome, however, goes beyond his depth in taking the position that his word is authoritative not only on matters of translation but also of canon, criticism, and exegesis of the kind that produces doctrine and theology. This exaggerated claim, like other peculiarities in Jerome's use of Scripture, could hardly have been recognized in its true light by the Middle Ages. Jerome was, in fact, rather an object for imitation, personifying the ideal of a Christian scholar in command of his literary sources (the Bible) and able to quote and adapt, and so to deliver the sacred text of long-hidden meaning, which he can then enlist to bring about Christian reform. What has actually happened is this: the passage of time had invested the fourth century with that same aura of authority and holiness that the fourth century had held toward Apostolic times. Jerome and the other great Fathers were thus endowed with a certain inviolability as vehicles in the continuing chain of revelation and tradition.

Temperament and Character

There is one final area that must be briefly touched upon, evident on the most superficial examination of Jerome's career and writing, yet difficult to substantiate. Although one must exercise extreme caution in assessing the psychological balance of great men solely on the basis of literary evidence, the question does have some direct bearing upon Jerome's career as a human-

ist. P. Steur has drawn up a sort of psychological check-
list as a control on Jerome's character,[33] and, more recently, Dr. Charles-Henri Nodet has published a lengthy
article on the degree to which Jerome's character and
temperament influenced his literary output.[34] Both studies draw heavily upon the corpus of the saint's writings
for their major evidence, and both are properly judi-
cious in their avoidance of the many pitfalls that could
arise from misreading the many commonplace references.

The conclusions arrived at by Nodet are of the most
interest in evaluating Jerome's contributions to humanism. Many scholars have already pointed out, apropos
of Jerome's dreams and temptations, that had the saint
eaten more decently and slept more regularly, he might
have fared better in his daily encounters with the noon-
day devil. Nodet delves deeper into the underlying psychology and finds Jerome's sexuality obsessive and re-
gressive. Evidence for this is his contempt for marriage,
his inability to fathom the meaning of conjugal love,
and the extreme nature of the advice he offers for the
preservation of chastity. His aggressiveness was strong
and poorly sublimated—witness the perennial irasci-
bility, the suggestive remarks, and the character of the
relationship he maintained with his few real friends.
Intellectually mature, he was sexually quite immature.
He was satisfied with a life of subtle dialectics, stub-
born and unsubtle in his thinking, drawing upon his
vast erudition largely for the permanent confirmation
of his own prejudices.

Now, these are damning judgments indeed, and they
are conclusions that we should be inclined to moderate,
in view of the above discussion, or simply even to dis-
miss as having little bearing on the discussion of humanism. There is, however, one significant point in a

study where vocabulary is of prime importance. Once again we must be aware of the facile assumption that words mean the same thing to everyone who uses them.

It is impossible not to note a certain equivocation in the specific vocabulary Jerome employs in his attacks upon sex, womankind, marriage, and things unascetical. He is using the same words that the theologian or master of spiritual direction uses, and to the casual observer, they appear to be the same: the vocabularies do in fact overlap. But there are fundamental variations in the formal approach. The language of the ascetic or spiritual director is objective, whereas that of Jerome is subjective and psychologically ridden with overtones and innuendos that inevitably but subtly vitiate the nature of the advice he is giving, so as to turn it into the projection of his own shortcomings and deep-seated fears. *Virgo*, for example, is a technical term in the vocabulary of the master of ascetic direction. In the earlier Roman vocabulary it was a less differentiated term, signifying maiden or marriageable girl or recently married young woman—*or* virgin. In the Christian context it is always laudatory, but in Jerome the word is all but an obsession. The same is true, in the inverse order, of *concupiscentia*, which always means evil desire.

We have already observed how Jerome could be unaware of the shift in connotative meanings of words, simply assuming they had always been the same for everyone whoever used them as they were in his own mind. He can thus construct what are to his mind telling arguments based on this material continuity in expression, and never realize the differences involved. It has been observed that men of considerable psychic energy, which should be applied to the totality of human living, when they focus it instead upon a rigidly circumscribed ascetical ideal, tend to overdevelop their verbal level of experience to the atrophy of their life experience. Thus words take on a life apart, like Plato's Ideas, endowed with a meaning, reality, and value all their own and capable, in the hands of a master, of enjoying an afterlife as well. Thus it is Jerome's vast influence upon the sympathetic audience of the Middle Ages that puts him in a unique position to contribute to the definitive setting of the laudatory and pejorative overtones of the Western Christian vocabulary—a fact unknown to the ages who accepted his authority so unreservedly. The people to whom Jerome addressed most of his work were men and women of the perfect or "desexualized" type, and it must be admitted that much of what he writes, if interpreted as bearing on upon the smaller community of the would-be elect, has considerable relevance. Even so, the pride of God's saints was visited upon Jerome long before their holiness. His reputation for being an uncompromising ascetic is owing more to a deep-rooted antisexual orientation and a morbid indulgence of neurotic insecurities than to any deliberate and manly sacrifice of something good for something better.

Although this conclusion can be easily overstated, the fact remains that the content and bearing of Jerome's writings were congenial to his spiritual descendants, the medieval monks who depended upon his teachings and shared his ideals. There is a deeper medieval attraction for Jerome that mere admiration and emulation of his classical erudition and literary brilliance. The position of the medieval scholar is easily appreciated. Scripture, and commentaries on Scripture, and the orthodox *opera* of the great Church Fathers were so much his literary and religious diet that the common words of the Bible (words that can be applied to philosophy or *humanistic* education before they become part of the specialized vocabulary for theology or Christian ascetical ideals) were so charged with new force of meaning as to overwhelm the medieval monk with their new message. After the long struggle with the secular clergy, the monks emerged victorious, and it was their ideals that formed the pattern for Christian aspiration and Christian humane education. The good words had all been preempted, and it was hard to find a spokesman for the other side—mere orthodoxy. The words heard by the Christian people were invested with a traditional authority, and their application extended equally well to the intellectual and to the spiritual spheres. Jerome is certainly not the only source responsible for the medieval state of affairs. No other single figure, however, serves as a point of convergence for so many streams of influence: mastery of Scripture, psychological bias, classical erudition, reputation for asceticism and holiness, champion of the monastic cause, role as spiritual adviser, mastery of words, and absolute quotability.

Jerome and Humanism

A humanist must have a wide appreciation of all of those *artes quae ad humanitatem pertinent*. Jerome really does not. Despite his boast of being *Ciceronianus*, Jerome has taken Cicero's way with words and has missed much of the fullness that Cicero gave to them, although he shares the humanist's enjoyment of words simply for their own sake. Aesthetic intuition is an integral element of classical humanism, and the Christian view in general, Jerome's in particular, is at variance with this fundamental attitude. Jerome's largely verbal level of involvement with the inherited ideals, moreover, precludes much of this fuller humanist perspective. He does indeed draw upon the past, and he does so for the sake of the present; but he misreads it by presuming a continuity of meaning in words and language. More fundamentally, he enlists the past to serve the present not as a model but as material to be subordinated to the building of a new edifice. This distortion dilutes, and even contaminates, the purity of his draughts from the fountain of classical pagan humanism.

Now, it is true that no Christian could have been entirely free of this failing, certainly not any Christian of the fourth century. Thus Jerome only shares a more fundamental attitude of the religion of his time—the tendency to make nature and human experience ancillary to the supernatural and to the prerogatives of grace. The Christian, even the Christian who had retained or rediscovered as much as was humanly possible of the legacy from the past, could no longer comfortably abide by such a large portion of its ideals as to accept classical humanism as a model for human endeavor, even upon earth and within the lesser span of man's terrestrial career. There was everywhere too little genuine formal continuity, too little trust, too great a hesitancy to focus upon the human or upon humanism. Ideally, as in Augustine's vision, the prospect of Christian man as a dilemma of warring worlds of flesh and spirit can be solved by granting each element its due, but the vision applied is less convincing. Historically, the Christian view of man is overly divinized. When Renaissance man appears, he is a sinner made to aspire after sanctity. The saints' lives became background for other, more human feelings, an admission of general inadequacy, a human pride at seeing some people achieve such lofty heights and the comfortable realization that this is not for all men. Goals and ideals were balanced with potential and experience in the rediscovered humanity that could be Christian without forfeiting man's capacity for humanism.

This did not happen in the fourth century, which not only missed something essential of what later Christianity was destined to develop into, but also directed its development along some awkward lines. It did in some measure prescribe the pattern for a future Christian humanism; and Jerome himself, though he did not draw everything he should have from the classical ideal and though he is guilty of demonstrable misdirection in his championing of the classical cause, did, for his time and age, represent a high degree of continuity with the classical culture.

One might be tempted to conclude that it is to the credit of the inherent vitality of both humanism and Christianity that the false avenues were eventually abandoned and the harm in large measure undone. I believe that Jerome, in the fourth century, had made a real beginning, for all his shortcomings, and an important beginning at that, in that it was in imitation and admiration of his humanistic learning that subsequent scholars were inspired to labor more successfully at the task of wedding Christianity and humanism in a cultural fusion whose ideals are still vigorous today. This is no mean accomplishment for the crotchety hermit.

The Renaissance has left us two distinct portrayals of Saint Jerome. There is Dürer's gentle recluse with the serene expression—the ideal of comfortable monastic formation. But there is also El Greco's picture of Jerome as the dark and troubled soul of medieval Christianity still searching for the vision of a Renaissance. If Jerome is too much a Christian, he is less a humanist for that. And if the Christian excesses of his asceticism are prompted less by a true appraisal of the Gospel challenge than by a certain imbalance, he does at least tower above the Middle Ages as the one paradoxical embodiment of Christianity and humanism: Christian to excess in the eyes of the Middle Ages and humanist to what they could only regard as perfection. What is lacking is the balance: Christian humanism must be something more than Christianity plus humanism or humanism plus Christianity. There must be a fusion that results in a new reality: *Christianus simul et Ciceronianus*. Insofar as this happy coalescence involves compromise and a vision of something that is both essentially new and essentially old, it is beyond the ken of Saint Jerome. His was the sterner task of perpetuating the individual elements without recognizing their potential. And although this is essentially a thankless task, surely we, who lay some claim to the profession of both Christianity and humanism, cannot ever be wholly without gratitude.

1. W. Jaeger, *Paideia: The Ideals of Greek Culture* 3 vols. (New York, 1939), 1 : 279. There are many definitions of humanism as a concept. We are concerned here not so much with the task of comparing or discussing their relative merits as with the work of isolating some of the more important elements and examining how they can or cannot be applied to the figure of Jerome and the fourth century.

2. This distinction and its consequences for the evaluation of history are discussed in greater detail by M. L. W. Laistner, *Christianity and Pagan Culture in the Later Roman Empire* (London, 1931; and Ithaca, N.Y., 1951); and *Thought and Letters in Western Europe A.D. 500 to 900* (London, 1931).

3. We must not overlook the ease with which the Roman philosophies and ethics, equally practical and moral in their orientation, fell in with the Christian moral Gospel. The community of interest was, in fact, so great that the *Moral Letters* of Seneca came to be regarded as Christian literature of a sort,

their author presumed to have been converted by Saint Paul in Rome.

4. The Christian draws not only from the Old Testament prophets but from Roman tradition as well. The Sibylline Books and the feeling for omens and auguries are easily Christianized. Witness Vergil's *paulo maiora canamus* and its devious interpretations over the Christian ages, and the express linking of the two streams of prophecy in the *Dies Irae: teste David cum Sibylla.*

5. *Sortes Biblicae* and *Sortes Vergilianae* made their way into the Middle Ages side by side.

6. Jerome's own writing, it must be noted, exhibits unqualified reverence for, and acceptance of, the status quo in scholarship and religion that are normally associated with the Christian tradition of a much later era.

7. This Christian intolerance is not always the result of deliberate and honorable concern for the purity of the Christian philosophy. It easily lapses into obstinate refusal to entertain, as a matter of principle, any alien sources of authority. In a man like Saint Jerome, this tendency is rather more in evidence.

8. The Church Fathers argue, for example, that revelation does indeed give insights into truths that would otherwise either be totally unknown, less accurately known, harder to acquire, or less surely believed in, and so on.

9. One could easily make the case that antiquity had also felt the need of similar reassurance. In the periods of decline from the classical ideal, we find a lack of direction and certitude that is generally called a failure of nerve, from the humanist point of view an apt enough term for a reaction that seeks to fix upon the metaphysical or transcendental. Christianity is sometimes made to appear as simply another of these mystery cults, like the later developments of Greek philosophy or Mithra, but there are some fundamental differences. There is a good historical survey of these trends in J. H. Randall, Jr., *Hellenistic Ways of Deliverance and the Making of the Christian Synthesis* (New York, 1970).

10. Cf. especially the Letters to the Thessalonians.

11. Exaggerated asceticism is the hallmark of the gnostic spirit as well.

12. H. Hagendahl, *Augustine and the Latin Classics*, (Stockholm, 1967).

13. One caution must be observed here: in their literary endeavor the Fathers are always essentially "more antique

Romans than the Christians." It is largely a question of degree: form and expression are never allowed to gain the upper hand.

14. The best introduction to this study is E. R. Curtius, *European Literature and the Latin Middle Ages* (London, 1952).

15. The position taken by E. K. Rand, for example, in his chapter on Jerome in *Founders of the Middle Ages* (Cambridge, Mass., 1928), fails to raise many important questions.

16. A. Lübeck, *Hieronymus quos noverit scriptores profanos et ex quibus hauserit* (Leipzig, 1872).

17. A good example is the *Treatise against Jovinian* (*AJ*), 1.41–49, with its catalogue of examples from antiquity, and 2.1–14, on the medicinal properties of certain foods and the dietary habits of various nations. These chapters have been extensively studied by E. Bickel, *Diatribe in Senecae philosophi fragmenta* (Leipzig, 1915), who makes a fairly convincing argument for charting their transmission to *AJ* via the agency of the now lost writings of Porphyry, a dependence never acknowledged by Jerome.

18. Letter 48, p. 13.

19. D. S. Wiesen, *St. Jerome as a Satirist*, Cornell University Studies in Classical Philology, no. 34 (Ithaca, N.Y., 1964).

20. Wiesen, chap. 7.

21. The terms of comparison are sometimes indelicate (*AJ* 1.4, 7), as is the reference to *incommoda nuptiarum* (Letter 22), or to sexual differences (*AJ* 1.36d), or to functions of nature (*AJ* 1.36b).

22. Apparent, for example, in the *Epodes* and earlier satire of Horace as it is influenced by Lucilius.

23. Juvenal develops this strain to perfection.

24. Some of the writing of Catullus is a good example of this usage in the hands of an unquestioned master.

25. *AJ* 1.8. The reduplication *cuius-eius* is also characteristic of translation from the Hebrew where the relative, being undifferentiated in case, gender, and so forth, requires the addition of a personal pronoun or a possessive adjective.

26. J. Marouzeau, *L'Ordre des mots dans la phrase latine*, 3 vols. (Paris, 1922–49).

27. There is a study on Jerome's use of clausulae by Sister Margaret Clare Herron, A.M., *A Study of the Clausulae in the Writings of St. Jerome* (Washington, D.C., 1937). The word order of the *Lives of the Desert Fathers* has been analyzed by

David F. Heimann, "Latin Word Order in the Writings of St. Jerome," (Ph.D. diss., Ohio State University, 1966).

28. This can be interpreted as the application of the techniques of verse writing to prose.

29. *AJ* 1.32. *Almah* is perhaps better translated as "girl of marriageable age," like the Latin *virgo*. Jerome is determined to defend the technical force of the word.

30. He defends this position in Letter 49.19 by appealing to the authority of Vergil, *numero deus impare gaudet* (*Écl.* 8.75).

31. The interpretation is further supported by a sort of natural-law argument derived from the Roman method of counting on the fingers. *AJ* 1.3.

32. Cf., for example, the formal Roman liturgical prayer, the Collect, which is constructed upon the most classical lines, observing great nicety in form, word positioning, and metrical cadence or *cursus*.

33. P. Steur, *Het Karakter van Hieronymus van Stridon Bestudeerd in Zijn Brieven* (Nijmegen, 1945). Other scholars have also discussed Jerome's character: Ch. Favez, "St. Jerome peint par lui-même," *Latomus* 16 (1957) : 655–71; F. Cavallera, "The Personality of St. Jerome," in *A Monument to St. Jerome* (New York, 1952).

34. Charles-Henri Nodet, "Position de S. Jerome en face des problèmes sexuels," in *Mystique et Continence*, Études Carmelitaines, no. 31 (Paris, 1952), pp. 308–56.

by Oskar Seidlin

IV

Goethe's *Iphigenia in Tauris:*
A Modern Use of a Greek Dramatic Theme

Let me start, in order to identify myself, with a very German question, a question that has worked a spiritual upheaval first in the country in which it was so insistently asked and that, eventually, was to redirect the whole course of Western civilization: How can I justify myself? To put it less theologically and dramatically: What am I doing here, and what gives me the right to be here? Am I just a guest from the outside, or do I belong here? I do belong—and not only for personal reasons—for men of Classics and I belong together, because there is no German spirit without the spirit of the classics; and whenever my home country's spirit reached its highest heights, it was anointed with a drop of sweet honey from Mount Hymettos.

Starting out by putting the shoe on the wrong foot, I want to remind my classical readers that they owe the German spirit a profound debt of gratitude, because surely they cannot forget the monumental contributions that Germany made to their discipline. Yet these contributions assuredly were nothing else but a loving, though modest, payment of the debt that Germany, the finest of Germany, owes to Greece and the Greeks. In the heroine's opening monologue of the greatest German classical play, Goethe's *Iphigenia in Tauris,* which I will discuss, the line rings out: "Seeking the land of

127

the Greeks with my soul"; and it is this search that has
haunted the German mind, the best of the German
mind, more powerfully, I think, than that of any other
nation from the earliest times, especially from the days
of Johann Joachim Winckelmann, who rediscovered the
greatness of Greek plastic art around the middle of the
eighteenth century, to the days of Nietzsche at the end
of the nineteenth, and well beyond.

But let me dwell for a moment at least, before I turn
to my subject, Goethe's *Iphigenia*, on Friedrich Hölderlin, the most exalted, intoxicated, and heart-rending
German traveler to Greece between Winckelmann and
Nietzsche, the purest vessel of the δαίμων of ποίησις, if
ever there was one. No, I am wrong; he was not a
traveler to Greece. What makes him so unspeakably
moving is the fact that, his heart and mind filled with
his love for the woman he called Diotima, he literally
saw Jupiter discharging lightning and rain over the tiny
garden patch in his Swabian village; and when he
watched the vintagers coming down from their vineyards
above the Neckar river, he took them for Dionysos
sweeping down the hills with his followers, all the Greek
Gods poised to set sail for his homeland, and he the
herald of their arrival, which would transform his poor
and barren Germany and make her the "holy heart of
all peoples." To be sure, it was madness, and in madness it had to end. But Hölderlin's insanity is the most
noble sacrifice ever offered by a nation upon the altar
of Greece, a price so precious that it fully pays for the
gift received.

There are some to whom this price seemed exorbitant
and this search for Greece so obsessive and misguided
that they diagnosed it as a positive disease and an
aberration of the German mind. For instance, an immensely intelligent writer of the recent past, the Eng-

lishwoman E. M. Butler, published a book thirty-five years ago entitled *The Tyranny of Greece over Germany* (the year was 1935, a time when, I am afraid, a very different tyranny held sway over that country), in which she claimed that Winckelmann's magic formula "noble simplicity and serene grandeur," by which he had tried to capture the spirit of Greek sculpture, had detracted the greatest German poets from their genuine essence and true destiny. She ends her fascinating presentation of Goethe, or rather should it not be called her fascinating settlement of accounts with Goethe, by proclaiming: "The potent spell of Winckelmann's Golden Age had proved a sinister one for Goethe. It had deflected the greatest Northern genius of modern times from his true and pre-destined bent."

I shall not argue against Miss Butler's thesis. I just want to cast a short glance at this "sinister spell" at its most potent in German literature, Goethe's *Iphigenia*, and, in so doing, address myself very modestly to the topic of ancient and modern use of dramatic themes. In no other instance of his entire literary production has Goethe so closely followed a canonical model, in this case the Euripidean tragedy, and yet given us, in his reworking of the ancient myth, so intensely personal and intimate a confession. By this I mean not only that a transmutation has occurred, which any of the old stories is bound to undergo when recast by a son of a later age, from Seneca to Jean-Paul Sartre, but that the given material has been infused with the spirit, the ideals, the demands, the hopes, and the despairs of his own times. Of course, Goethe's *Iphigenia* is a document of the intellectual climate of his period, and very decidedly so. It *is* the reflection of a guardedly optimistic, enlightened humanitarianism as it could emerge only at that particular place in Europe and at that particular moment in European history. But underneath it is—and we may, indeed, call this a modern use of a Greek dramatic theme—a direct projection of the poet's very personal and very unique existential problem and condition: curse-laden and curse-driven Orestes is Goethe himself, in the anguish of his heart, pursued by the furies of his own restlessness and uncontrollable tensions; Iphigenia, both sister and beloved, is the woman he met in Weimar, who by her strength, patient endurance, and purity was to lead him back to his lost and forfeited "home" and to lift the curse that he felt to be his inexorable inheritance. This is not only an old myth in a modern dress but a handed-down, again-and-again transformed story as a vessel of the most intimate personal confession.

It was perhaps this intense personalization of the ancient theme that induced Schiller, Goethe's most perceptive and intelligent critic, to call his friend's Greek play "astonishingly un-Greek." Right he was, and for another reason as well, a reason that, at first glance, seems to contradict what I have just said about the eminently confessional character of Goethe's *Iphigenia*. No matter how poignant a projection of his own emotional travail, his play is at the same time a conscious formulation of the human condition as such. And here we encounter, I think, another modern use of a Greek dramatic theme. Even though the great tragic writers of Greece rendered in their tragedies situations and constellations that were generally applicable to, and seen as, manifesations of man's fate, they did, it seems to me, consider their fables a presentation of a specific human case or a specific human situation, often linked to identifiable local establishments, cultic establishments of the Greek οἰκουμένη—as, for example, Pallas Athena's inauguration of the Athenian Areopagus in Aeschylus' *Oresteia,* or the veneration of the statue of Delphian Artemis to which the Iphigenia material is linked. By this I do not want to suggest even faintly that the Greek writers ascribed historicity to the events of and in tragedy. It was, after all, Aristotle who drew a sharp dividing line between history and μῦθος, when he defined, "History relates what, let us say, Alcibiades did or suffered, poetry represents the general, and this consists in how a human being of a certain character is likely or compelled to speak and act." A human being of a certain character—this given individual—this "case"; and I think cases, sensational and often gory, were given to us in all the reworkings through the centuries, psychologically or psychopathologically enriched as in Racine's *Phèdre* or O'Neill's *Mourning Becomes Electra,* interlaced with the author's personal philosophy or the intellectual temper of his age as in Voltaire's *Oreste* or in Alfieri's *Agamemnon,* or used as vehicles for some timely political concerns as in Werfel's *Trojan Women,* Girardoux's *La guerre de Troie n'aura pas lieu,* or Anouilh's *Antigone.*

Goethe's *Iphigenia* is different. He presents her story as what we today would call archetypical in the strictest sense, not only speech and action of a certain character under a set of given circumstances, but as a projection of the *condition humaine* per se, the breaking through of man into his authenticity. It may very well have been this redirecting of an ancient dramatic theme that made it possible for a great anatomist of the human soul, coming a little over a century after Goethe's classical play, to discover in Sophocles' *Oedipus* the most powerful ancient dramatic theme, the basic and unchangeably valid pattern of every son's position between his father and his mother, a conception that I venture to guess, is far from what the old Greek legend had even remotely in mind. And what Goethe did with the Iphigenia material is, so I believe, equally far removed from what the ancient story had in mind.

What he did with it amounts, indeed, to the search for, and conquest of, man's authenticity, and it is for this reason that his whole play centers around the discovery and the confession of truth. The play celebrates that which alone can lift the curse imposed upon us by suprapersonal forces, by the inexorable decree of the gods: the veracity of man's existence, his breaking through the shell and the snares of an unalterable determination into the recognition of his autonomous substance. Exactly in the middle of the play, at its very center—and center here is not simply an indication of place—Orestes, facing the unknown priestess of Artemis, Iphigenia, who does not know him either, exclaims: "Between us twain be truth. I am Orestes." At first glance, this may seem no more than the standard scene of recognition—ἀναγνώεισις the Greeks called it—that forms one of the high points of so many Greek tragedies. But it is, in the case of Goethe's *Iphigenia*, much more than that. It is not only, as in the Euripidean tragedy, the moment when the two protagonists reveal their identities to each other; it is, rather, the moment of truth: Orestes cutting through the veil of deceit, of inauthenticity, with which he, or to be exact his friend Pylades, had shrouded his very existence by making Iphigenia believe that he was not who he really is. What Orestes lives through here is an agonizing act of confession, because by naming himself, he names and confesses his unspeakable crime, the murder of his mother. It is this confession, this making himself known, that is the beginning of his recovery and of his liberation from the suffocating grip of guilt and corrosion.

"Between us twain be truth"—Iphigenia, Goethe's

Iphigenia, could repeat these very same words when she faces King Thoas and informs him of the deceitful stratagem that with her consent, has been hatched against him: the theft and abduction of the statue of Taurian Artemis and the surreptitious flight of the three Greeks. It is a confession fraught with mortal danger—and Iphigenia is fully aware of it—because the irate king could easily destroy her, her brother, and his friend. Again, the moment of truth has come, the demand to assert and confess one's own verity, no matter how deadly the risk, no matter how cruel the price this truth may exact. It is at this point that Goethe has strayed decisively from his model, for the act of Iphigenia is a clear defiance of the god Apollo, who had ordered her brother to travel to the land of the Tauri and to bring back to Greece the statue of his sister-goddess Artemis languishing in the barbarian land. Yet Iphigenia, fully aware of the god's decree and of the promise that its execution holds for her brother, for herself, and for her whole house, will—at the critical moment—thwart the fulfillment of the divine command because to her it is inconceivable that the gods want a deed carried out that involves deceit, betrayal, and trickery.

In Goethe's version Iphigenia's courage to recognize and speak the truth, her own and that of the situation in which she finds herself, has the farthest-reaching ramifications. After she has broken through to the very core of her personal truthful existence, and *only* after she has done so, the truth of the gods, the true meaning of their will, stands revealed. As it now turns out— and this is Goethe's most radical departure from the ancient version of the fable—Apollo, when ordering Orestes to bring home the sister, was not thinking of his own sister, Artemis, but of Orestes' sister, Iphigenia.

This reinterpretation of the divine oracle and its fulfillment may seem no more than a bit of dramatic sophistry designed to assure a happy ending, which will include, besides the three Greeks, the barbarian king as well, who, losing the beloved priestess of Artemis as he must, will at least keep the hallowed statue of the goddess. Yet, it is, of course, more than that. It is proof of the Goethean conviction that only when and after man has found and professed his authenticity, the divine is free to speak truly and to announce the very meaning of its will. The act and triumph of self-recognition, of discovering one's veracity and very substance extends, beyond the human sphere, to the godhead itself.

To be sure, this is a twist astonishingly un-Greek, a radically modern use of an old theme in which the dramatic action as such, the events of the myth, are no longer of primary importance as Aristotle had insisted they should be, but the whole play is turned into a paradigm of the process that leads to man's self-awareness and self-realization. And as such, as a catalyst in the experiment of discovering one's own truth, Goethe experienced all themes, dramatic and otherwise, that Greek poetry had bequeathed to mankind; exactly the opposite, it would seem to me, of what Miss Butler diagnosed as a "potent spell" deflecting one's true and predestined bent. Late in his life, in one of his many general maxims, Goethe explained of what use the ancient Greeks were to him, and it is exactly this use that he had made the very topic and action of his own Greek play. He offers this clarification in the form of a little imaginary dialogue that runs as follows: "Someone said to me: 'Why do you trouble yourself so much with Homer? You can't really understand him anyway.' To this I answered: 'Neither do I understand sun and moon and stars; yet they are passing over my head and

I recognize myself in them while gazing up there, and doing so I wonder whether perhaps, one day, I might amount to something, too.' " To recognize oneself so that one day one might amount to something, too—this means, indeed, putting the ancient themes to new and good use. Upon reflection, such an attitude may be the most desirable outgrowth of that self-critical spirit that developed in Greece during her most glorious period. In any case, it is answer and echo of the admonition that was inscribed on Apollo's temple in Delphi as the highest task the god of light and poetry had assigned to man: γνῶθι σεαυτόν.

by Harry C. Rutledge

Classical Latin Poetry: An Art for Our Time

*tum canit, errantem Permessi ad flumina Gallum
Aonas in montis ut duxerit una sororum,
utque viro Phoebi chorus adsurrexerit omnis*
—Vergil, *Sixth Eclogue*

This essay is a broad discussion of the artistic climate of our times and of the possible meaning of classical Latin poetry for these times.[1] The view presented is a broad one, for I have come to have an increasingly eclectic appreciation of literature and the whole "world of art,"[2] and to see that world as a unity. I hope to show my concern for the immediacy, the pertinence, of classical Latin poetry for our time. I want to discuss Roman poetry of the "Golden Age" as it both affects and is affected by our life today. Though I shall restrict myself to illustrations from the poetry of the late first century B.C., a similar presentation could be made of other classical literature. In order to see how Roman poetry is related to the artistic climate of the twentieth century, in particular to the present artistic climate of the United States, we need to examine the nature and the composition of this climate. Obviously, we cannot examine the present without a consideration of a number of its artistic and cultural antecedents. No discus-

136

sion of the American artistic climate would be complete without a consideration of our European connections. To begin, let me suggest that the work most characteristic of the temper of this century is the novel by Thomas Mann, *Doctor Faustus*. This complex work intertwines the history of the Devil-beset musician, Adrian Leverkühn, with the rise and fall of Nazi Germany. Employing that total awareness of history and adroitness of narrative that we admire so much in Vergil, Thomas Mann weaves together a picture of Germany in Adrian's lifetime (the first part of this century) with Germany during the Second World War. In addition, Thomas Mann depicts Leverkühn's development as a modern artist whose work resembles that of Arnold Schönberg.[3] The climax of the story comes in the scene where Adrian has invited his friends to a private recital of his new oratorio *The Lamentation of Doctor Faustus*. To the consternation and horror of the assembled party, Adrian proceeds to confess his past sins and his compact with Satan. The scene concludes with the following passage in which Adrian is speaking: [4]

"But since my time is at an end, which aforetime I bought with my soul, I have summoned you to me before my end. . . . I beseech you hereupon, ye would hold me in kindly remembrance. . . . All this bespoke and beknown, will I now leave to play you a little out of the construction which I heard first from the lovely instrument of Satan and which in part the knowing children sang to me."
     He stood up, pale as death.
     "This man," in the stillness one heard the voice of Dr. Kranich, wheezing yet clearly articulate: "This man is mad. There has been for a long time no doubt of it, and it is most regrettable that in our circle the profession of alienist is not represented. I, as a numismatist, feel myself entirely incompetent in this situation."

> With that he too went away.
>
> Leverkühn, surrounded by the women, Schildknapp, Helene, and myself, had sat down at the brown square piano and flattened the pages of the score with his right hand. We saw tears run down his cheeks and fall on the keyboard. . . . He spread out his arms, bending over the instrument and seeming to embrace it, when suddenly, as though smitten by a blow, he fell sidewise from his seat and to the floor.

The collapse of Adrian Leverkühn is dramatic and sensational. There are those readers who might find it extravagant. In fact, however, the fall of Adrian is just as logical and is prepared for as thoroughly as the fall of Oedipus in *Oedipus the King,* Phaedra in *Hippolytus,* Pentheus in *The Bacchae,* or Dido in the fourth book of Vergil's *Aeneid.* The scene is dramatic in the grand classic style, but though we could find further parallels in classical Greek literature, it is only in Roman poetry that we have in the Latin language the display of such a tragedy as that of Mann's novel. Before I pursue, however, the significance of Roman poetry in comparison with modern literature, or before I claim too strongly that Adrian Leverkühn is symbolic of our age, let me describe the world of art that we have today and then relate the poetry of Rome to this world.

It has been the age of "the nightmare cry of Dada." [5] As Calvin Tomkins has observed, Dada, a movement that began about 1916, was "first and foremost a revolutionary state of mind, a violent assault on all accepted values." [6] A product of the First World War, Dada produced in its adherents the feeling that "these humiliating times have not succeeded in wresting respect from us." [7] This attitude, expressed by Hugo Ball, a German conscientious objector, is one that we have repeatedly heard in recent years. The world situation has improved very little since 1916, and the arts are still in a revolutionary state; thus we are still hearing the cry of Dada. Many of us may not realize it, but we are living among Dada's reverberations today, which at least partially accounts for what appears to be the continuous decline of the still widely admired cultural and artistic values of the eighteenth and nineteenth centuries.

The advent of Dada signaled the withdrawal of the creative artists of Europe and America from the Cult of Beauty. The world was rotten, and it was the task of art to reflect that world. The high priest of Dada was the painter Marcel Duchamp, who was capable of putting a mustache and goatee on a reproduction of the *Mona Lisa* and of entering a toilet fixture, signed by himself, in an art exhibit.[8] More serious and more prolific was Pablo Picasso, whose shocking and hideous pictures of women painted in the 1930s show his own disenchantment both with the state of affairs in Spain and in a Europe plainly headed for a holocaust.[9]

It was in the 1940s that Paris and London ceased being the art capitals of the Western world and New York assumed her present regal ascendancy. It was in New York during the forties, after the outbreak of the Second World War,[10] that the painter Jackson Pollock developed the expressionism of such European artists as Wassily Kandinsky and Oskar Kokoschka into painting for the sake of painting, "action painting."[11] With the unveiling of Pollock's *Blue Poles* in 1953, the requirement that painting should be representational was declared null and void. This picture, a major example of the new megalography (Monet's water lily sequences are among the first such specimens of modern art), is energy and action on canvas; it is color and dynamism for themselves, because there is nothing that is solid in the painting except, perhaps, the dancing "blue poles" themselves.

Blue Poles and Dada are related, and both, as suggested by my reference to Monet, have origins in the years prior to 1916. We are unrealistic if we fail to recognize the central position in the history of this century, and in this century's artistic and intellectual temper, that is held by the First World War. Here in 1972, it is very clear that the massive and complex problems that have beset the world since 1930 all stem from older issues that were germinating before the First World War and were not settled by that conflict. It has been a century, seven decades so far, of revolt and rebellion. The mold of European civilization that began with the reign of Caesar Augustus and continued until the reign of Edward the Seventh, though punctuated by such major developments as the rise of Protestantism, the collapse of the monarchy in France, and the Industrial Revolution, remained, in a remarkable way, the same. In this world the powerful and the obedient were easily distinguished. In the arts, for the most part, accepted taste and artistic direction were set up by the people of wealth and culture, who took their example and standards from the noble heyday of Athens, Rome, Florence, and Paris. The Cult of Beauty, as would have been understood by both the Platonists and the Neo-Platonists, was supreme.

There were a few vocal critics of this universal standard. The most notable, I think, was the Marquis de Sade, whose works are a negation of normal Western standards. To the Marquis de Sade the universally admired human being who is imbued with physical beauty combined with a sense of morality, meant nothing. But the works of de Sade were banned for more

than a century after his death in 1814 and had little
overt influence until recent years.

More widespread criticism of the standards of the
past and serious concern with its burden began in Europe in the 1880s. In painting, it has been suggested,
the revolt is marked by the work of Paul Gauguin,
whose *Jacob Wrestling with the Angel* (1888) is like
no picture seen before in Europe [12] (at least in the nineteenth century), because neither its form nor its ico-
nography has any immediate significance for the observer. The revolt against tradition and the old Cult
of Beauty that Gauguin had begun was advanced especially by Matisse, who as a leader of a new group of
artists nicknamed *les fauves* brought painting even further away from traditional representation.[13]

Today, with the perspective and scholarship of sixty
years to help us, we can see how radical and influential
Matisse's paintings of the 1910s were, particularly the
two-dimensional *Harmony in Red* (1908–9) and those
deceptively simple pictures, now in the Hermitage,
Dance and *Music* (1910). These extraordinary innovations in painting were paralleled in music by Stravinsky's *The Rite of Spring,* performed for the first time in
1913.[14]

In literature there began at the same time a similar
reaction to the social standards of the past and a questioning of the old presentation of the human condition,[15]
a presentation related mainly to the aristocracy or upper bourgeoisie. The new spirit is shown most strikingly
by two novels, Robert Louis Stevenson's masterpiece *The
Strange Case of Dr. Jekyll and Mr. Hyde* (1886), and
Oscar Wilde's *The Picture of Dorian Gray* (1891). Stevenson makes a probe into human nature, and Wilde
criticizes the leisured class with a severity that is totally
at variance with the depiction of life found in earlier

Victorian work. Nothing could be farther removed from
the attitude of such a high Victorian work like Trol-
lope's *Barchester Towers* (1857) than Wilde's *Dorian
Gray*. Jackson Pollock and all the members of the "New
York School" could only approve of those seminal observations in Wilde's preface to his novel: "All art is
at once surface and symbol. Those who go beneath the
surface do so at their peril. Those who read the symbol
do so at their peril. It is the spectator, and not life, that
art really mirrors." "All art is quite useless."

It was, however, the First World War that launched
irrevocably the cultural and aesthetic revolution in
whose whirlpool we are still struggling. The First World
War, we can now see clearly, brought about "the death
of Europe." [16] It was, furthermore, after 1918 that,
slowly but surely, the cultural center of the West began
to shift from Paris and London to New York. Paris, of
course, continued to be an important center, though in
the 1920s it was the Americans in Paris—Gertrude Stein
and her circle, Hemingway, and the Fitzgeralds—who
were a dominant element. After the Second World War,
Paris once again assumed something of her old influence
and position, especially in philosophy. The recently
published diaries of the American musician and Fran-
cophile, Ned Rorem, describe a postwar Paris that is
attractive, though the elegant circle of the Countess de
Noailles has much of the genteel tone of Mme de Vion-
net's group in James's *The Ambassadors*. Missing is the
exuberance of Gertrude Stein and of the earlier *belle
époque*. In painting the work in France of both Matisse
(who died in 1954) and Chagall was still of the greatest
importance. But since the Second World War, no city
has had such advantages from municipal and private
patronage of the arts as New York City. In my opinion
New York is today what Rome was in the age of Herodes

Atticus and the Antonines; London and Paris are in the position of Athens in the second century A.D. It was the emigration of European intellectuals and scholars and the first prominence of the "New York School" of painting in 1940 that made our "new Rome" and this country the active heirs of an exhausted Europe.

More fundamental, however, than this transfer of cultural leadership and authority from one city to another was the irreparable damage that was done to traditional values by the catastrophe of the First World War. Only gradually has the damage been understood. In 1959 Hugh Kenner could refer to "the death of Europe." In 1971 nobody would quarrel with Walter Kerr's statement that "the back of our world has been broken, we have heard the snap, whatever we see as we turn the next corner will in itself be as bizarre as a Bosch or a Swift could wish it." [17] It has taken us fifty years to recognize and understand that the standards of the nineteenth century, represented primarily by unquestioning acceptance of vested authority whether in government or art, have become moribund.

One artist who saw clearly what was happening and appreciated the changes, however unhappy, that were taking place before his very eyes was T. S. Eliot; the work, *The Waste Land*, published in 1922. With this major poem Eliot anatomized the state of the postwar West and demonstrated that literature, too, was about to go the way of painting and music. (Literature is ever the most conservative of the arts.) The literature on Eliot is almost Vergilian in proportion, and I have listed in an earlier essay some of the more penetrating and helpful critiques. [18] Moreover, it is not my intention here to do more than remind you of the importance of Eliot as critic and observer. Like Vergil, like Janus, Eliot looked behind and ahead in the sharpest possible way in his poetical description of the state of Europe, the "death of Europe," in *The Waste Land.*

This utterly engrossing, fascinating poem reflects, and yet breaks with, the past; it blends the historical past with the historical present; it freely combines the majestic mythological prophet Tiresias with a pathetic stenographer and her coarse "young man carbuncular"; mixes such grandiloquent phrases as "The Chair she sat in, like a burnished throne" with the lingo of the music hall "Well, if Albert won't leave you alone, there it is, I said, / What you get married for if you don't want children?" And through it all we move from the awesome death wish of the Sibyl at Cumae, in "April . . . the cruelest month," to an expression of both hope and grace: "I sat upon the shore / Fishing, with the arid plain behind me / . . . Shantih shantih shantih."

It seems to me that *The Waste Land* is the most original and modern work of art of the century.[19] In this poem there are representations of ordinary life and the use of ordinary language (one is reminded of the novel use of unelevated language in the poems of Lucilius and Catullus); at the same time there are gorgeously colored descriptions (the burnished throne and the church of Magnus Martyr) worthy of Chagall or Stravinsky. There are violent transpositions that are like the switching of channels on a television set or the multisensory narrative of a modern novel like William Burroughs's *Naked Lunch* (1959), or the jagged streaks and flashes of paint employed by the expressionist painters. And in the dramatic scenes that deal with vulgar life so theatrically, there are the seeds of episodes found later in the plays of Tennessee Williams and Edward Albee.

On the other hand, though Eliot's work is typical of the creative work of the twentieth century and though there is much that is strikingly novel and wonderfully immediate for the social and intellectual mood of "the years *l'entre deux guerres*," Eliot proves in *The Waste Land* that the burden of the past need not be intolerable, that the past very much has its still important uses. Throughout this century, at least since 1910, all too many writers and artists in the other arts have been weighed down by the burden of the past and, in a wild-eyed search for novelty, have often succeeded in producing only what is ephemeral. As W. Jackson Bate observes in discussing the intellectual malaise of the eighteenth century in England, there are many similarities to be found in that era and our own. Today there is the same attraction to primitivism, a search for "escape from drab complexity into color and vigor, the yearning for simplicity," the presence of "fatigue and depression that so often seem to accompany success." [20] The careers of F. Scott Fitzgerald, Eugene O'Neill, Tennessee Williams, and Ernest Hemingway, among others, illustrate the last point particularly. The present widespread concern with world conditions and the retreat of countless young people into a primitive and simple way of life are documented facts. The arts of today plainly "mirror the greatest single cultural problem we face, assuming that we physically survive: that is, how to use a heritage, when we know and admire so much about it, how to grow by means of it, how to acquire our 'identities,' how to be ourselves." [21] Eliot clearly and cogently, more definitely than other modern artists who continued to be influenced by classicism, for example, either Picasso or Yeats, has shown us "the present-day vitality of the classical tradition," [22] and he demonstrated this vitality in his superbly original *The Waste Land*.

The fact remains, however, that although Eliot's modern idiom has been very influential, his classicism has

been little imitated. And so today, we find ourselves
agonized by the classical languages' "melancholy, long,
withdrawing roar." Many artists will not tolerate the
burden of the past; many devotees of the classics are
only too like Thomas Mann's Dr. Kranich, the numis-
matist, who found himself appalled by the *furor* of
Adrian Leverkühn and went away, feeling himself entirely incompetent in this situation.

But I would suggest that Greco-Roman literature, especially Roman poetry, has never been more pertinent.
Indeed, I know of no time besides the present, except the
age in which the poetry was written, when Roman poetry has had more to say to humanity, or when the conditions of society would allow a deeper, more honest, and
open appreciation of the subject matter of classical
Roman poetry.

It is a commonplace of the classroom that in modern
art we have a return of "Alexandrianism," and that the
esoteric nature of such poems as those of Cummings,
Eliot, Stevens, and Yeats, or paintings like those of
Willem de Kooning, recall the private approach to art
employed in the last three centuries before Christ. I
have no doubt that Apollonius and Lycophron would
comprehend the method and the manner of modern poetry; the later Hellenistic artists, especially the sculptors,
would understand the problems involved in abstraction,
whereby the plastic arts are pushed to their very limits.
Both eras have experienced novelty produced for the
sake of novelty, art for the sake of art. It is easy to see
T. S. Eliot, with all his learning, invention, and authority, as the new Callimachus.[23]

To be more precise, we need to see that many of the
characteristics of the years from 1910 to the present are
very like problems and attitudes prominent in the first
century B.C. Some of these problems and attitudes are:

the widespread sense of futility and despair, of helplessness; the passion for novelty; a yearning to escape; an egocentrism or fascination with the self that borders on a sentimental self-absorption. Particularly prominent then and now is the hatred of war, an attitude to which so many patriots have in their turn violently reacted. In addition, as in the Hellenistic sculptors' representation of the sensual (whether Aphrodite or a drunk old woman) or the writers' depiction of the tormented (whether Catullus's Ariadne or Vergil's Dido), so in recent years have we beheld the utterly candid presentation of human nature. The stage has offered particularly conspicuous examples of this new candor, beginning, we might say, with Ibsen's *Hedda Gabler* (1890), continuing with O'Neill's *The Great God Brown* (1926), and later in Williams's powerful *A Streetcar Named Desire* (1947), Friedrich Dürrenmatt's *The Visit* (1956), and Edward Albee's *Who's Afraid of Virginia Woolf* (1962).[24]

We find ourselves today, I venture to suggest, with a greater understanding of human nature and a greater compassion than have been generally exhibited in any other age. The experience of the past sixty years, the age of Thomas Mann, Sigmund Freud, Mahatma Gandhi, and T. S. Eliot, has made our era particularly receptive to the famous line of Terence: *Homo sum: humani nil a me alienum puto* (*Heauton Timorumenos* 77). And we can also assent more knowledgeably than our ancestors to Vergil's line: *Sunt lacrimae rerum, et mentem mortalia tangunt* (*Aeneid* 1. 462). The experience of the last sixty years has given many of our writers a remarkable understanding of the vagaries of the human condition and a sense of tragedy that hitherto were the special attributes of observers like Thucydides in the late fifth century and Vergil in the late first century B.C.

The world of classical Greece, especially the ages of Homer and Pericles, has always had a great immediacy and pertinence. For this reason Greek studies have always been more popular, more fashionable, than Latin studies; and Greek literature has always seemed to be easier to teach than the literature of Rome. It was in 1939, with the publication of Sir Ronald Syme's *The Roman Revolution* (one of the most illuminating and influential studies in the classics completed in this century), that the world of Rome, particularly the first century B.C., began to be seen as an age remarkably like our own. In our own country several pioneering historians and literary scholars have complemented Syme's work: among others Bernard M. W. Knox, Paul MacKendrick, Lawrence Richardson, Jr., and Lily Ross Taylor have been Ariadne leading us through the labyrinth of Roman history and literature. With their help we have come to a state of revelation, in seeing how very similar to our own were the values and problems of the first century B.C.[25] As was the case for Aeneas when he came to the mural in the Temple of Juno that depicted his past in the Trojan War, so too have we experienced the shock of recognition.

To be more specific, though we would be wrong to attempt to draw exact parallels, we have come to see how very maladjusted society was in Italy in the first century B.C. The economic depression of the 1930s and the outbreak of World War II resemble similar situations in the first century B.C. The people of wealth, privilege, and selfishness (or public irresponsibility) were present in classical Rome as well as in the Russia of Nicholas II, or in Harding's America, or in the Weimar Republic. The desire of people of an inferior social and economic status to improve their lot, as in the cases of Spartacus and his band or some of the followers of Catiline, resembles a similar longing seen in recent decades in this country, in Germany, in India, and in Africa. The "new deal" of Caesar Augustus and the "welfare state" that he inaugurated bear resemblances to the regimes of both Franklin D. Roosevelt and Benito Mussolini. It was the perspicacious Syme who first stated in plain language the ways and means of Caesar Augustus.[26] Not that this revelation should spoil our appreciation of the Augustan accomplishment. That world was so sick that it could not get any worse, and only drastic remedies could possibly help.

For the literary critics, the candid view exercised by Syme in 1939 was reinforced by the new approach to the criticism of poetry as advocated particularly by John Crowe Ransom in his *The New Criticism* of 1941. Soon thereafter, classical scholars began to be interested in Greek and Roman poetry as pure poetry, without such a strong emphasis as before on the biographical, sociological and historical aspects of the poems.

Of course, it is a coincidence that the year 1940 is a pivotal one for classical scholarship, literary criticism, and the beginning of the "New York School" of painting. We might also regard 1940 as a very important one for our arch-poet, T. S. Eliot, considering that his play *The Family Reunion* (based on *The Oresteia*) was published in 1939; "East Coker," the second of the *Four Quartets,* appeared in 1940, with the work concluded by "Little Gidding" in 1942.[27]

What we have here, in the years around 1940, is a combination of circumstances that began quite separately but became related. The rise of fascism, the continuing influence of the Dada movement, the widespread yearning for a truly original development in art, the need for a new approach in literary criticism, all were circumstances of the 1930s that, it appears to me, were accentuated and pushed into maturity by the new collapse of Europe in 1939–40. I would not want to say that the war was the only catalyst for these rumbling intellectual movements. Certainly, however, Eliot's *Four Quartets* owe not a little to the state of Europe at that time; the *furor* of Germany and her resulting agony are at the heart of *Doctor Faustus;* and the world at war gave abstract expressionism a new impetus and a new validity. Very like the first century B.C., this century has been a time of chaos and flux, for years on end. Yet, out of the confusion and the rubble, some remarkable works of art have emerged. Whether these works will prove to be as significant for their own age and for the future as the *De Rerum Natura,* the *Aeneid,* or the "Laocoön" remains to be seen. Moreover, our international conflicts have not come to a definite conclusion as did the conflicts of the first century in 31 B.C. Nor has the new Augustus yet appeared.

Nevertheless, our era is strikingly similar to the earlier Hellenistic Age both in political circumstances and in artistic trends. Both eras have been caught up in a passionate enthusiasm for artistic novelty and originality; in both periods there has been an obsessive fascination with the individual personality; both centuries have brought men to a deep appreciation—owing to intimate experience—of tragic occurrences and tragic developments.

Let me illustrate briefly how particularly interesting in the 1970s are some works of literature from the Golden Age of Rome. I want to point out the modern character of these works both in attitude and in pertinence, and to suggest that the temper of our times is ideally suited to the proper appreciation of some of these Roman works that have not always been well received or properly understood. My illustrations will be from the poetry of Horace, Lucretius, and Vergil, but not the brilliant and ever appealing Catullus, whose novel contributions have been discussed by so many critics, notably Kenneth Quinn in his *The Catullan Revolution* (rev. ed., 1969).

Turning first to Horace, whose delicate, subtle, richly suggestive, tantalizingly allusive poems now support the weight of almost innumerable critical essays and books, I will refer only to one poem, the first Ode of the Fourth Book:

> Intermissa, Venus, diu
>   rursus bella moves? parce, precor, precor.

"The wars of love . . . spare me Venus, I beg you spare me." Published in 13 B.C., when Horace was fifty-two, the poem and the book it introduces appeared at the apogee of the reign of Augustus, the year the Senate voted the erection of the Ara Pacis. This poignant unsparing poem knows no peace. The poet begs the relentless mother of Love (*mater saeva Cupidinum*) to work her ways on a young man, one who (ingenuously) wants to be in love. By such a worshipper, Venus will find herself richly honored by the Alban Lake in a shrine of citron wood. But the poet knows only too well that this goddess is "la belle dame sans merci"; and, besides, "I grow old . . . I grow old." [28]

The last two stanzas, the final eight lines of the poem, are among the most quiveringly sensual, disarmingly poignant lines in all Latin poetry:

> Sed cur heu, Ligurine, cur
>   manat rara meas lacrima per genas?
> cur facunda parum decoro
>   inter verba cadit lingua silentio?
> nocturnis ego somniis

iam captum teneo, iam volucrem sequor
te per gramina Martii
campi, te per aquas, dure, volubiles.

"But, but why, oh why, Ligurinus, does a tear now and then slip down my cheek? Why does all my brilliant talk suddenly stop, indiscreetly? In my dreams at night one moment I hold you fast, in the next I pursue you racing over the field of Mars and then, unyielding one, through rushing waters."

In 1911 Lord Dunsany, the translator of the *Odes* for the Everyman's Library edition (1961), refused to deal with the last eight lines of the poem saying: "As a convinced Unionist and, usually, an admirer of Horace, I am very reluctant to prefer Mr. Gladstone to him, but I do so on this one occasion, and I follow Mr. Gladstone in not translating the unpleasant last lines of this ode." [29] We are, for the most part, past that stage; and in the modern climate that takes love as love, just as it was in antiquity from Sappho to "Longinus," we can deal with Horace's poem today honestly and as it deserves.

The poem is typical of the quicksilver mind and art of Horace in which several views are always simultaneously entertained. Steele Commager's analysis of the poem is generally as penetrating and understanding as is his treatment of other odes. I do not think, however, that Horace for one moment is the conventional *miser amator* in this poem. Commager's own reversal a few lines later brings him to the truth when he says, "The overwhelming sensuousness of the final image irretrievably banishes not only Horace's earlier excuses but the whole atmosphere of stylized complaint as well." [30] Whether or not this poem reflects Horace's own experience has no bearing on our appreciation of the poem. But certainly the poem can be taken as the perfect expression of loveless man at middle age, whether the person be Horace, Gustave von Aschenbach (*Death in Venice*), or Blanche Dubois (*A Streetcar Named Desire*). Horace's poem deals with human nature with all the understanding and honesty that characterize more recent writing, and I am thinking particularly of the work of Conrad Aiken, Edna St. Vincent Millay, and Dylan Thomas. The terms *posture* and *convention* are contemptible ones today. Although there is much artifice in the poetry of the Augustan period, particularly in the work of Ovid and Tibullus, the great writing, full of art, rises above artifice; and Horace is one of the great writers.[31] His sometimes humorous, sometimes serious, but always accurate delineation of the human condition is just as compelling today as it was in the first century B.C.

Horace's poem begins with a reference to Venus and ends with the Field of Mars. Venus and Mars, Love and War, Love and Death. Let us move backward in time to Lucretius, whose incomparable poem begins with the famous invocation to Venus and ends with a description of the merciless plague at Athens in 430 B.C. In Lucretius's deep concern with the physical world, in his quest for knowledge, in his passion to understand everything, and in his scientific humanism, he is one of the most modern of ancient authors, though only quite recently has his work begun to be understood.[32] In Lucretius's pursuit and praise of the dynamic and the concrete, of action, choice, and commitment, in his zeal for the authentic and his denunciation of unauthentic existence, he is the most compelling "existentialist" of all the classical poets and philosophers.[33]

It is his passion for reality and rationalism and the honor he pays to the physical world that make Lucretius important to the modern reader. It is in Lucretius that we come to feel the distinction between "sensuous" and "sensual," because though Lucretius loves the physical world, he despises lust.[34] In his poet's desire to depict Life, he equates Life with Venus herself in his prologue (1. 1–49). Thereafter, Lucretius generally avoids mythological analogues in order to keep to the facts of Life. His praise of decent marriage is plain (4. 1195–1224). But in his love of *ratio* Lucretius hates *furor* in any form and so despises sensual self-indulgence (4. 1073–1191).

As an observer of the phenomena of life, Lucretius is unsurpassed. What finer, sweeter observation is there than his pertaining to evaporation and the gradual dissolution of hard objects:

> denique fluctifrago suspensae in litore vestes
> uvescunt, eaedem dispansae in sole serescunt.
> at neque quo pacto persederit umor aquai
> visumst nec rursum quo pacto fugerit aestu.
> in parvas igitur partis dispergitur umor
> quas oculi nulla possunt ratione videre.
> quin etiam multis solis redeuntibus annis
> anulus in digito subter tenuatur habendo,
> stilicidi casus lapidem cavat, uncus aratri
> ferreus occulte decrescit vomer in arvis,
> strataque iam vulgi pedibus detrita viarum
> saxea conspicimus; tum portas propter aena
> signa manus dextras ostendunt attenuari
> saepe salutantum tactu praeterque meantum.[35]

Such a joy in life! "Wet clothes, the familiar ring grown thin, the iron plow in the earth, the hand of the statue repeatedly touched by the faithful." The sixteenth century was not without such appreciations, nor was the nineteenth; but the fervent directness of Lucretius fits in especially well with the attitudes of the twentieth. If the passage just quoted needs any elucidation at all, I should do so with a poem of Richard Wilbur, "Love Calls Us to the Things of This World," which has these excited lines:

> "Oh, let there be nothing on earth but laundry,
> Nothing but rosy hands in the rising steam
> And clear dances done in the sight of heaven." [36]

Sensuous, but not sensual. Lucretius's poem is antithetical to that part of the modern mood typified by the work of Henry Miller. That there are many admirers of Henry Miller, but even more of his idiom, cannot be denied. But in other writers what appears to be the Milleresque spirit is deceptive. The greatest literature of recent years, though concerned with the sensual, more often than not contains, in fact, a plea for rationalism and control.[37] The parable is obvious in the story of Adrian Leverkühn and his pursuit of the Hetaera Esmeralda. Those who feel that *Lady Chatterley's Lover* is the model for our liberated era should reread the very end of the book, Mellors's letter to Constance, and notice how Mellors really advocates the temperance and the achieving of a beauty in physical love that is supported by Lucretius in Book Four of *De Rerum Natura*. The tragedy of the hedonistic Gatsby in F. Scott Fitzgerald's famous novel has always been apparent. The wretchedness of the flamboyant Scott and Zelda Fitzgerald themselves, partially due to their voracious hunt for pleasure, has recently been drawn with new clarity by Nancy Milford in her biography, *Zelda* (1970).

Lucretius is unflinchingly and relentlessly honest. His description of life is perfectly faithful to the facts. There is no delusion, no sham in his poem. He depicts the cycle of creation and destruction. The description of death in the form of the plague, at the end of the poem, is simply a truthful conclusion of Lucretius's "Hymn of Life." It is not, however, a discouraging ending; the careful reader will realize that the cycle will begin anew immediately. On the other hand, it is certainly true that one leaves the poem with a sense of humility and an appreciation of moderation as the natural principle of all human action.[38] Man will be foolish; life is tragic; but the cycle of life goes on. At the end of *Doctor Faustus*, though we are filled with pity for the unhappy Adrian, there is one consoling thought: his music will be immortal. *Non omnis moriar.*

And so to Vergil, the most Roman of Latin poets, whose masterpiece the *Aeneid* has an extraordinary immediacy for us and our times. It is Vergil's works that most fully reflect the turbulence in both art and life of the late Hellenistic Age. Thus in the parallels that I have worked out between the first century B.C. and the twentieth century A.D., it is Vergil to whom I have been leading as the most classical of poets, the one that is of constantly universal interest.

I cannot possibly do justice to Vergil in only these concluding pages. The Vergilian bibliography has become impossible for one person to master; but it is noteworthy that some of the most influential studies have appeared in the last ten years: Viktor Pöschl's, as translated into English in 1962 (originally published in German in 1950); Brook's Otis's in 1963; Michael Putnam's in 1965; and Kenneth Quinn's in 1968.[39] As I observed earlier, it has been since the publication of Syme's *Roman Revolution* (1939) that we have begun to take a searchingly honest view of Augustan Rome and to analyze the real, the underlying feelings of the writers of that period. Our own disillusionment that began at the end of the Second World War has deeply affected our study of the arts. Many critics and scholars can work only with the feeling quoted previously of the German conscientious objector Hugo Ball: "These humiliating times have not succeeded in wresting respect from us." It has been in recent years, then, that the melancholy of our condition has made many critics acutely sensitive to any such pessimism in the works of the Greek and Roman writers. In the face of so much divided public opinion on the issues of our time, we have become deeply conscious of, and sensitive to, "the outsider," with the result that it has occurred to many of us, I am sure, to write supplementary essays for Colin Wilson's famous book so as to include such ancient figures as Achilles and Aeneas, Euripides, Catullus, Vergil, and Propertius. All these figures might well answer the question in Wilson's Shavian epigraph, "You feel at home in the world then?" with a reply "(from the very depths of his nature): No." [40]

Vergil has three memorable characters who represent his poetry at its essence and who have a symbolic value for both Vergil's time and ours: Tityrus, Orpheus, and Aeneas. Tityrus, whom we see as a benevolent shepherd playing a flute at the beginning of the *First Eclogue,* is all of us who, by some virtue or by the grace of authority, are spared the more difficult involvements, decisions, and agonies of life. He is Lucretius's philosopher standing in his isolated tower as life surges about him (*De Rerum Natura* 2. 1–4); he is Horace in his *reducta valle* (*Odes* 1. 17. 17); he is Matisse rejoicing in life despite life. Tityrus is perfectly aware of the arid plain behind him and has seen London Bridge falling down; still, today, he sits upon the shore (cf. *The Waste Land* 424–27).

Orpheus, whose entrancing yet appalling history is the end of the *Georgics,* is Adrian Leverkühn. Here is the artist, seeing all and suffering everything, who dies in torment but whose work transcendently survives.[41] Orpheus, Adrian—here is Man, in our century, enduring more than any character of Kafka and not really understanding why he should deserve such punishment. In the passionate, innovative, anguished lives of Hart Crane, Jackson Pollock, Dylan Thomas, and Virginia Woolf, we have had Vergil's Orpheus among us in recent years. As after Adrian's death in any asylum, we remember the music, so in Orpheus's violent death we remember the music that caused Hell itself to stand still (*Georgics* 4. 481–84).

The *Aeneid* is the supreme artistic achievement of the Hellenistic Age. It embodies the literary and artistic ideals and goals of the last three centuries before Christ. At the same time, Vergil fulfills his desire, announced in the prologue of the third book of the *Georgics*, to give up novelty for the sake of novelty. In the *Aeneid* Vergil does create a classical masterpiece equal to such Greek classics as Homer's *Iliad*, Aeschylus's *Oresteia*, and Sophocles' Theban cycle. Vergil's dream of erecting a marble temple—a regular Parthenon—beside the Mincius River in Roman Italy (*Georgics* 3. 12–18), before which he will parade as a triumphant charioteer, that sublime dream, is realized in his epic poem.

The passionate actions, richly colored backgrounds, highly individualized portraits, frustrated love, a world in turbulence, a highly charged atmosphere of tragedy— all these attributes of Hellenistic art, the same attributes of the great art of our time, are found in the *Aeneid*. In the first six books are particularly sharp reflections of the artistic climate of Vergil's day, the climate of late Hellenistic art. It was a climate that favored highly original uses of traditional forms, whether the forms of Homer or of Callimachus (from the second of whom

Vergil was removed by more than two hundred years). The *Georgics* are a model production of that late Hellenistic taste. With the *Aeneid*, however, Vergil brought late Hellenistic art to its highest possible development.

There is nothing in ancient literature to equal the color, the flash, the sustained atmosphere of excitement, and the swift but impressive action of the first six books of the *Aeneid*. Here is Vergil's most arresting contribution to literature, and here Vergil excels the great and original contributions made by Catullus in the epyllion of poem 64 as well as his own tour de force in the Aristaeus epyllion at the end of the *Georgics*. Vergil's narrative art has never been excelled, and subsequent European literature owes everything to Vergil. In the *Aeneid* we have the consummate achievement, the ultimate show of originality, the *Blue Poles*, of the Hellenistic Age. Borrowing everything from the past, as do Mann, Joyce, and Eliot, like these writers Vergil goes on to achieve the height of originality and to give a new direction to art as did Picasso, Matisse, and Jackson Pollock.

Let me, however, recall some of the particularly Hellenistic features of the poem. For one thing, Iopas's song of the seasons (1. 740–46) recalls the work of the great Alexandrian scientist-poets Aratus and Eratosthenes. In Book 2, the Laocoön scene (2. 199–233) seems to be based on the famous statue itself, which, though possibly not in Rome as yet, Vergil undoubtedly knew by reputation. Dido, whose melodramatic background we hear of in Book 1, is a superbly composite figure whose great scenes come in Book 4. She is at once Clytemnestra, Medea, and Phaedra from classical Greece; but Vergil's rendering of the Tragic Queen, the *domina infelix*, would have been impossible without Apollonius's Medea and Catullus's Ariadne (Poem 64).

In Book 6 Hellenistic science and philosophy are briefly but distinctly acknowledged in Anchises' speech to Aeneas describing the workings of the universe. Vergil's indebtedness to Lucretius is clear time and time again.[42] Behind all the dramatic action of the first six books looms the shadow of the Rome and the Italy that are to be (just as in Eliot's *Waste Land* and the *Four Quartets*, there are always present London and England). This great emphasis on City and Society, on the undeniable fact of man's membership in a society, is a particular contribution of Vergil to late Hellenistic literature; and it is this contribution that makes Vergil's *Aeneid* such a substantial bridge between antiquity and modern times.[43]

Anchises' speech about the universe and the life of the soul owes as much to Plato as to Lucretius. The end of the Sixth Book, with its depiction of the future glories of Rome's Italian past and her Augustan present, leads us from the Odyssean first half of the poem to its Iliadic denouement. Here Vergil recovers and creates anew (in Latin at the end of the Hellenistic Age) the atmosphere of Homer's war-torn plain and its proud reckless leaders; here anew and just as poignantly is the keening of the *Trojan Women;* here is a man—so much an anti-hero—as tortured and beleaguered as Orestes but with as fixed and determined a purpose as Oedipus. Vergil re-creates and infuses with a special Italian vitality the sense of tragedy, the presence of tragedy, that characterize Greek classicism.

It is the character of Aeneas to which we today can particularly respond. Whereas there is starkness, and thus the two-dimensionality of a vase painting, in such figures as Achilles, Hector, Oedipus, and Phaedra, there is in Aeneas all the complex roundness of a Hellenistic statue. We are constantly aware of his many sides and thus find him both as fascinating and as elusive as a portrait by Picasso in which the sides of the face are presented all at once. The technique of modern fiction that combines conversation, the inner thoughts of the conversants, and the narrator's analysis, has become a familiar one. This achievement of literary three-dimensionality can be seen in the later novels of Henry James, certainly in Joyce, and, later, in Virginia Woolf and Lawrence Durrell. We watch Aeneas, we hear him speak, we learn of his thoughts that are contrary to his words, we hear others describe him. Only gradually does the whole man appear, and there are surprises in his character even at the end of the poem. We never really know the complicated Aeneas any more than we know anyone else. In addition to this complicated characterization, there is Vergil's method of freely blending the past with the present—Agamemnon's Greece, primitive Italy, and Augustan Rome. There is the poet's highly subjective handling of his characters (as Brooks Otis has described so well); and there is the complicated web of allusions both to literature and to history. This depiction of man in his every facet has been one of the important innovations in the writing of this century, with a most Vergilian example to be seen in John Fowles's novel, *The French Lieutenant's Woman* (1969), in which some characters of Victorian England are carefully observed from our point of view.

Of course we would expect the complexity of modern life, often nightmarish, to be reflected in contemporary art. The presence of the past, our awareness in recent years of the whole world, the ubiquitous conflicts among cultures, our educational system that will often bring a young mind into contact with Cambodia and Nigeria before it really has come to grips with, shall we say, Rome or Boston—the kaleidoscope that is the modern world—is to be found, though perhaps on a smaller scale, in the world of Vergil. Aeneas the wanderer, committed to a cause he only gradually understands, forced to move from one world to another, hungry for peace and rest but unable to find either one, passionate yet dutiful, sluggish yet ambitious, eager to please but determined to hold his own—Aeneas is the kind of complex man whom the twentieth century has produced in equally complex circumstances. Vergil's representation of such a multifarious world with all his allusions, his flashbacks, his acceptance of contradictions, actually anticipates the modern approach in the novel, the film, and in poetry.

At the end of the epic Aeneas stands over the dead body of Turnus, whom he has killed. Turnus is a tragic figure, but he is tragic as Pentheus is, not Oedipus. His determination to assert himself, to go against the wishes of King Latinus himself, is his tragic flaw. A careful reading of the three great prophecies in the poem (1. 257–96, 6. 756–892, 8. 626–728) shows that Vergil did believe in the greater good to be realized from the union of Trojans and Latins, and that the death of Turnus did not mean the destruction of the world of Italy, that world of wilderness combined with pastoral order. Moreover, when you step back from the poem and consider it as a whole, you see that Aeneas did not succumb to the forces of violence and irrationality.[44] The death of Turnus is not a triumph, but a regrettably necessary solution.[45]

With Aeneas we leave Adrian; in Aeneas we have a greater man. Our own anguished and disillusioned times, of which Adrian Leverkühn is especially symbolic, have, however, seen occasionally and with favor a *pius Aeneas*. In addition to several living men there has been Celia Coplestone and her search for satisfaction in Eliot's *The Cocktail Party;* there has been the nobly self-effacing Seymour in the tales of J. D. Salinger; there has been the old poet Nonno and his song of courage in Williams's play *Night of the Iguana*. To have the bravery, the loyalty, the perseverance, the ultimate selflessness of Aeneas; the determination to make the best of adversity and to unravel the ambiguities all around us; to love something and to be zealous in the pursuit of that love—many of us have had such aspirations. On the other hand, the breathtaking turbulence and challenges of the twentieth century have made us all familiar with the similar exasperations, despair, and cloudy triumphs of Aeneas.

It is in the world of art that we find our problems and our selves defined. The description, delineation, and explication provided by the poets, novelists, sculptors, and painters of this century are unusually sensitive and exact. For some of the answers, at least, we need only to be aware and to look, because much understanding is to be found in the world of art. We need not, however, end our questioning and our search for clarification in contemporary works. There is an equally valid and cogent understanding of life in the work of the poets of classical Rome.

1. I am indebted to Mr. David Heimann, of the University of Colorado, for help in planning this essay, and to Mr. Frederick Nicklaus, of the Columbia University Press, for his criticism of the completed draft.

2. The phrase is stimulatingly used by Henry Steele Commager in his *The Odes of Horace* (New Haven, Conn., 1962) as the title of chapter 6.

3. Thomas Mann, *Doctor Faustus: The Life of the German Composer Adrian Leverkühn as Told by a Friend*, trans. H. T. Lowe-Porter (New York, 1948), p. 512. All subsequent references are to this edition.

4. Ibid., p. 503.

5. Calvin Tomkins and the Editors of Time-Life Books, *The World of Marcel Duchamp* (New York, 1966) p. 55.

6. Ibid., p. 57.

7. Ibid., p. 56.

8. Ibid., p. 39.

9. For commentary and representative selection of reproductions see David Douglas Duncan, *Picasso's Picassos* (New York, 1961). Picasso initiated the revolution in painting against traditional values and the Cult of Beauty as early as 1907 with his *Les Demoiselles d'Avignon.*

10. Thomas Mann had come to New York earlier, in 1936. Bela Bartok the composer came in 1940, as did a large group of painters. Concerning the *emigré* artists, see Bryan Robertson, *Jackson Pollock* (New York,1960), pp. 66–71; Hilton Kramer, "30 Years of the New York School," *New York Times Magazine,* 12 October 1969, p. 28.

11. Robertson, *Jackson Pollock,* p. 36.

12. Henri Dorra, *Years of Ferment: The Birth of 20th Century Art* (Los Angeles, 1965), pp. 9–10.

13. There are many studies on this subject, but Dorra, *Years of Ferment,* pp. 26–36, presents an excellent summary.

14. An adequate cultural history of the twentieth century may be an impossibility; there are so many threads to be both separated and brought together. A step in the right direction is Barbara Tuchman's synthesis of the years 1890–1914, *The Proud Tower: A Portrait of the World before the War* (New York, 1966).

15. Of course this movement began earlier, and it has been frequently discussed. Flaubert's *Mme Bovary* (1857), condemned at publication, later enjoyed a *succès de scandale.* Only recently have the novels of Charles Dickens come to be regarded as the masterpieces of social criticism that they are. See Steven Marcus, "Dickens after One Hundred Years," *New York Times Book Review,* 7 June 1970, p. 1. Henry James entered the fray in 1886 with his *Princess Casamassima* (for the best evaluation see Lionel Trilling's essay in *The Liberal Imagination,* [New York, 1950]), the same year in which Stevenson published *Dr. Jekyll and Mr. Hyde.*

16. Hugh Kenner, *The Invisible Poet: T. S. Eliot* (New York 1959), p. 143.

17. Walter Kerr in a review of *Cymbeline, New York Times* 23 August 1970, sec. 2, p. 1.

18. "Eliot and Vergil: Parallels in the Sixth *Aeneid* and *Four Quartets,*" *Vergilius* 12 (1966) : 11–20.

19. Though Joyce's *Ulysses* appeared in the same year, it is not so strikingly original a work of literature as it at first might seem. Certainly, the famous "stream-of-consciousness" technique can be found to have its antecedents in certain passages in such advanced novels as James's *The Golden Bowl* (1904).

20. W. Jackson Bate, *The Burden of the Past and the English Poet* (Cambridge, Mass., 1970), p. 47.

21. Ibid., p. 134.

22. This phrase was the title of a conference sponsored by the American Council of Learned Societies at Indiana University, 22–23 January, 1958. The papers presented there have been collected and edited by Whitney J. Oates, *From Sophocles to Picasso: The Present-day Vitality of the Classical Tradition* (Bloomington, 1962).

23. Cf. J. K. Newman's epilogue "Alexandrianism in Modern English Poetry" in *Augustus and the New Poetry*, Collection Latomus 88 (Brussels, 1967), pp. 437–54.

24. Of course the novel, the major art form of our century, has lately manifested the same candor, particularly with the decline of censorship that began with the publication by Grove Press in 1961 of Henry Miller's *Tropic of Cancer*. But the novel is an art form to be enjoyed privately. The new candor in the theater and in the film is a more conspicuous example of the new attitude.

25. See, for example: L. R. Taylor, *Party Politics in the Age of Caesar* (Berkeley, 1949); Paul MacKendrick, *The Mute Stones Speak* (New York, 1960); L. Richardson, Jr., *Poetical Theory in Republican Rome* (New Haven, Conn., 1944) and "*Furi et Aureli, comites Catulli,*" *Classical Philology* 58 (1963) : 93–106; B. M. W. Knox, "The Serpent and the Flame: The Imagery of the Second Book of the *Aeneid,*" *American Journal of Philology* 71 (1950) : 379–400; Kenneth Quinn, *The Catullan Revolution* (Melbourne, 1969); Victor Pöschl, *The Art of Vergil,* trans. G. Seligson (Ann Arbor, Mich., 1962). The debt of American scholars to scholars abroad such as the Vergilians Pöschl, Heinze, Norden, Skutsch, and R. D. Williams is plain, but one point of the present essay is to emphasize America as the "new Alexandria" or (better in the context of the westward movement) the "new Rome."

26. For two appreciative observations of Syme's radical new treatment, see the reviews of W. L. Wannemacher, *Classical Weekly* 34 (1940) : 18–19; and A. F. Giles, *Classical Review* 54 (1940) : 38–41. On the similarity between the first century B.C. and the present one, see L. R. Taylor, *Party Politics in the Age of Caesar,* p. 1.

27. It is noteworthy here and pertinent to the latter part of the present essay (as related to Vergil's development) that Eliot's work became increasingly classical, both in manner and in significance. Eliot's movement from the romanticism of alleys, rose gardens, and retreats of the alienated individual to a classicism that insists on the relation of art to life is well traced by Marion Montgomery, *T. S. Eliot: An Essay on the American Magus* (Athens, Ga., 1969), esp. pp. 26–29, 90–97.

28. T. S. Eliot, "The Love Song of J. Alfred Prufrock," from *Collected Poems, 1909–1935* (London, 1936), p. 15.

29. Lord Dunsany and Michael Oakley, trans., *The Collected Works of Horace* (London, 1961), p. 91.

30. Commager, *The Odes of Horace*, p. 294. But even recent criticism has its blind spots. It is hard to see how anyone could regard these concluding lines as an "amusing surprise-ending" as does the usually helpful Gordon Williams, *Tradition and Originality in Roman Poetry* (Oxford, 1968), p. 557.

31. A corrective is offered by David West's *Reading Horace* (Edinburgh, 1967). His observations on how the Soracte Ode "has been destroyed by the critics" (p. 3) and reduced "to a shambles" (p. 8) are a little strong since, in fact, one finds himself easily forgetting the criticism but never forgetting the poem. The most helpful of contemporary critics have been Commager, *The Odes of Horace*, and Eduard Fraenkel, *Horace* (Oxford, 1957). For West's sensible remarks on *Odes* 4.1 see pp. 134–36.

32. D. E. W. Wormell, "The Personal World of Lucretius," in *Lucretius,* ed. D. R. Dudley (New York, 1965), p. 35, explains why Lucretius *ought* to appeal to the modern reader. But the fact is that until recently many teachers have not understood Lucretius's art, as made clear by Richard Minadeo, *The Lyre of Science: Form and Meaning in Lucretius's "De Rerum Natura"* (Detroit, 1969), pp. 9–11 and n. 16, p. 114.

33. For these terms of definition see Maurice Friedman, *The Worlds of Existentialism: A Critical Reader* (New York, 1964), pp. 3–4. Once again, however, the classical authors are practically unacknowledged. In Friedman's group of "Forerunners" he includes only Heraclitus.

34. Cf. Wormell, "The Personal World of Lucretius," p. 57.

35. C. Bailey, ed., *Lucretius, "De Rerum Natura"* (Oxford, 1947), ll. 305–18.

36. *Things of This World* (New York, 1956), p. 5. Wilbur's poem is a good parallel for the simple, straightforward passage

from Lucretius. If one wanted to pursue Lucretius's "existentialism" and use deeper modern parallels, of course, he would want to refer to the work of Rainer Maria Rilke, particularly to *Das Stundenbuch* (Leipzig, 1905), repr. in vol. 2 of *Gesammelte Werke* (Leipzig, 1930). Rilke's poetry is both "expressionist" and "existentialist" and, therefore, closely related to the artistic developments of this century; but the present essay, as a mere sketch of twentieth-century trends, can only emphasize the more obviously influential figures and works.

37. Most interesting is the change from devotee of Miller to stern critic made by Lawrence Durrell as shown in *A Private Correspondence* ed. George Wickes (New York, 1963). Of Miller's book *Sexus*, Durrell writes: "The moral vulgarity of so much of it is *artistically* painful" (p. 265). Of Jack Kerouac and other such writers whom Miller admired, Durrell is compelled to say: "They need a week at a French lycée to be taught to think and construct" (p. 348).

38. Minadeo, *Lyre of Science*, p. 110.

39. Victor Pöschl, *The Art of Vergil*, trans. G. Seligson (Ann Arbor, Mich., 1962); Brooks Otis, *Virgil: A Study in Civilized Poetry* (Oxford, 1963); Michael C. J. Putnam, *The Poetry of the Aeneid* (Cambridge, Mass., 1965); Kenneth Quinn, *Virgil's Aeneid: A Critical Description* (London, 1968).

40. Colin Wilson, *The Outsider* (Boston, 1956), p. ii. The epigraph is from Bernard Shaw's *John Bull's Other Island*, Act IV.

41. Brooks Otis, *Virgil: A Study in Civilized Poetry* (Oxford, 1963), pp. 190–214, is splendid on this. Cf. my note "Vergil's Daedalus," *Classical Journal* 62 (1967) : 309–11.

42. Cf. Wormell, "The Personal World of Lucretius," pp. 64–65, and n. 23, p. 69, in which he cites the earlier researches of Bailey and Merrill.

43. Michael Putnam, *Virgil's Pastoral Art: Studies in the Eclogues* (Princeton, N.J., 1970), has interesting remarks (esp., p. 393) to make on the presence of Rome in those poems. Unfortunately Putnam allows the same oddly negative interpretation of the world of Rome to intrude as he showed in his *The Poetry of the Aeneid*, a book that has made a number of other critics view the *Aeneid* as being on a "long day's journey into night." Our own harsh times and ruinous wars have at least partly prompted the pessimistic views of these critics, whose works are the ultimate extension, as it were, of Syme's presentation of Augustus.

44. Putnam, *Poetry of the Aeneid*, p. 192.

45. It would not be appropriate to give here a detailed study of the character of Aeneas. Essentially my understanding of Aeneas at the end of Book 12 is that of Brooks Otis, *Virgil: A Study in Civilized Poetry*, pp. 380–81.

by Kenneth M. Abbott

Epilogue

These papers reflect some of the widely varied interests of the scholar to whom they are dedicated. The topics thus may seem to differ widely and the views expressed, as was to be expected and indeed welcomed, to diverge as well. Still, as was to be hoped for, the affirmations that underlie all of them do not really differ. Professor Seidlin need hardly defend himself against a suspicion of being among the alien corn. The great Greek revival in Germany has never struck classicists as lying outside the boundaries of their proper interests. That it does lie outside the boundaries of professional competence of the classicist is quite another matter, and although a number of us did read Goethe's *Iphigenia* in college for comparison with Euripides, at least one of us is now thankful for a clearer understanding of it. Indeed, far more classicists tend to feel that the fourth century is more alien than Goethe, and a large number of those in the humanities have for some years regarded the twentieth century as a disaster area best avoided by those who wished to escape corruption of their taste. Yet all

169

these papers in different ways and not by design have demonstrated, in the affirmations that underlie all of them, the continuities in spite of the disruptions and the essential vitality of the classical tradition. All the papers, then, even if illustrating at times what Robert Frost called the truths that are in and out of fashion, have as their point of reference their firm adherence to the truths that men keep coming back to. And they have kept coming back to them when they realized, as the English philosopher Austin once said, "Importance isn't important; truth is," though few in the United States in the present century would venture to state as flatly and as succinctly as the director of the Ashmolean Museum recently did, that "in this world the useful exists for the sake of the useless."

There is, to be sure, a divergence in conclusion between the papers of Professor Babcock and Professor Rutledge on the one hand and Professor McDonald on the other, on the question that has pressed upon all of us with increasing urgency, which is to say, the hopes for the future of classical learning. That the classics in Greek and Latin have survived disasters in the past and have risen from the dust there is no dispute. That the themes and concerns of the first century B.C. are not alien to the twentieth century Professor Rutledge has thoroughly shown. Yet Professor McDonald's paper challenges the assumption that the current crisis of the humanities in general and the classics in particular will in its turn pass away. His position is a reasoned one, based on his unfailing respect for evidence. He has not needed to show at length that we and the whole Western world are in an unhappy period; it has seemed to some at times in human history that man was little lower than the angels, but at other times, and the latter half of the twentieth century is one, man has impressively extended the distance. The culture of the twentieth century no longer seems to please more than a few of its customers, and one could save a good deal of the paper squandered in the law school at Yale on this subject by saying that a very great many of more thoughtful men would agree in essence with the father in *Sabrina Fair,* "I have lived in the twentieth century . . . as long as any man and longer than most. And I feel I know as much about it as the next man . . . The twentieth century! I could pick a century blindfolded out of a hat and get a better one!"

No doubt neither Professor McDonald nor any one of the rest of us would take quite so dangerous a gamble unless the third century and the fourteenth century after Christ were removed from the hat—ages that compiled an impressive record of human misery, although possibly not quite so much mindlessness and mendacity as are now our daily experience in public discussion. Yet the third and fourteenth centuries were followed by the fourth and fifteenth centuries, not only by fixed numerical habit but by impressive human endeavor, and the men and women of those periods accomplished much and rebuilt much. In his thorough examination of that first and crucial renaissance to which we owe so much of what it preserves for modern man, but which we so often regard as merely a period of transmission, Professor Heimann does well to remind us of elements of discontinuity in the fourth century, and Professor Rutledge is right in urging us to look with more sympathy and understanding at our own century.

Yet it seems hard to deny that the present prospects for the humanities are not bright. Professor Babcock has done well and worked diligently to try to set within an intelligible framework, for which a definition is not yet possible, the voices of dissent. If I understand his discussion, the New Humanism, if it is humanism in any sense we can recognize, is a discontinuity of the sharpest kind, if indeed it is not a counter culture that loses all meaning when it cannot be in opposition. No one, in any event, is likely to maintain that some kindly act of providence will save us. Yet those human efforts, as in Avianus's fable of putting one's shoulder to the wheel of the mired cart in collaboration with help from on high, have been and are being made. Surely, we can give our aid, remembering, as Heraclitus noted, that "the eyes and the ears are untrustworthy witnesses when the soul is barbarous".

Notes on the Contributors

Mark Morford is professor of classics and chairman of the Department of Classics at the Ohio State University.

Charles L. Babcock is professor of classics and formerly chairman of the Department of Classics at the Ohio State University.

William F. McDonald is professor emeritus of history at the Ohio State University.

David F. Heimann is assistant professor of classics at the University of Colorado.

Oskar Seidlin, formerly the Regents' Professor of German at the Ohio State University, is professor of German at Indiana University.

Harry C. Rutledge is professor of classics and head of the Department of Classics at the University of Tennessee.

Kenneth M. Abbott is professor of classics at the Ohio State University.

173

Index

Aeneas, 160–63; anguish of, 163; complexity of character of, 160–62; and death of Turnus, 162; virtues of, 163. *See also Aeneid*

Aeneid, 138, 147, 150, 156, 158–60, 162; as Hellenistic poem, 156, 158–60; narrative art of, 159; pertinence of, for twentieth century, 156, 159, 160. *See also* Vergil, Aeneas

Afterlife, in Christian humanism, 83–86, 94

Alexander the Great, 35, 36

Alexandria, as literary center, 36; and Alexandrianism, 146

Antique: distinguished from classical, 62–63; language, 109; society, 103

Apollo, 133, 135

Arendt, Hannah, 6–7

Aristotle, 33, 34, 37, 45, 134; definition of history and poetry of, 131; system of philosophy of, 70

Art: in America, 137, 142–43, 165 n.24; Hellenistic, 146–47, 150, 158, 160; modern, 138–40, 141, 145, 159, 163; in twentieth-century Europe, 138–40

Arts and Sciences, colleges of, 7, 50–51, 54

Asceticism, 80, 84–85, 118–19, 120, 124 n.11

Athens, 33, 60

Augustine, Saint, 42–43, 45, 84, 87, 95, 121; *City of God,* 62, 89; *Confessions,* 62, 89, 91

Augustus, Emperor, 140, 149, 151

Bryn Mawr College, 25

Butler, E. M., *The Tyranny of Greece over Germany*, 129, 134

Catholicism, 31, 32 *See also* Church, Catholic
Charlemagne, 43, 44
Christian Fathers, 62, 73, 95, 116; attitudes toward the classics of, 42, 86–92, 124 n.13; education of, 42; faith and philosophy of, 75, 77, 124 n.8; use of Scripture by, 111
Christianity, 28, 30, 43, 54, 75–77, 83, 85, 103, 122–23; and the classics, 28–29, 31, 32, 43–44, 46–47, 49, 53–54, 57, 63–64, 70, 86–88, 90–92; and gnosis, 80–83; and Judaism, 30; medieval, 122; modern, 49, 60; Roman, 60; and Roman religion, 72–74, 124 n.4
Christ-Janer, Arland F., 8
Church, Catholic, 43, 48, 49; and education, 43–44, 46, 49; history of, 81; male-dominated, 103–4
Cicero, 17, 33, 35–39, 40, 42, 66, 100, 120; *De Officiis*, 15, 35; *De Oratore*, 33, 37–39; *Pro Archia*, 24
Clark, Christine Philpot, 25
Classical languages, 13, 36, 51, 146. *See also* Greek, Latin
Classicism, 109; Christian, 30, 31, 57, 86–88; in T. S. Eliot, 145–46, 166 n.27; Greek, 160; pagan, 92
Classics, 23–24, 52, 66–67, 146, 170; as basis of civilized culture, 48–49; and

Christianity and humanism, 28–57 passim; in Germany, 127–29, 169; as humanities, 15; *in extremis*, 28; in interdisciplinary studies, 23; and New Humanism, 3–27 passim; and patristic writings, 86–92; and sciences, 19, 21, 22–23, 28; subsumed by English departments, 56; subsumed by non-Christian culture, 55; survival of, 55–57; in translation, 13, 14
Commager, Henry Steele, 10
Commager, Steele, 152
Common Life, Brethren of the, 32–33, 41
Communism, 50
Compendia: in antique culture, 63; and Jerome's writing, 89, 98–101
Composition: art of, as basis of education, 34–35; in Jerome, 105–10; in Latin literary tradition, 68–69

Dada, 138–39, 149
Declamatio, 41, 90
Duchamp, Marcel, 139
Dunsany, Lord: declines to translate Horace, 152

Education: American system of, 9–10, 23, 29, 161; Christian, 29, 30–33, 43–44, 44–47, 50, 120; Cicero's theory of, 37–39; Greek, 33–35, 36; higher, 11, 33, 36, 44, 51; humanistic, 12, 17, 20–21, 26, 49, 53–54, 119; Isocrates' theory of, 33–35; Jesuit, 31–33, 41; liberal,

7–8, 10, 25, 34, 38, 40, 48, 61; mass, 50; medieval, 38, 44–46; and morality, 34–35, 47, 53–54; Renaissance, 42, 47–48; Roman, 36–42, 100; secondary, 11; and society, 23, 35–36, 44, 45, 48–49; specialization in, 21–22, 52–53

Eiseley, Loren, 19–21

Eliot, T. S., 143–46, 149, 166 n.27; *The Cocktail Party*, 162; *The Family Reunion*, 149; *Four Quartets*, 149–50, 160; *The Waste Land*, 143–45, 157, 160

Else, Gerald, 15

Erasmus, 46–47

Euripides: and Euripidean tragedy, 129, 132; *Trojan Women*, 18, 160

Exempla, 98, 101; in Jerome's writing, 89, 98–99, 103

Freud, Sigmund, use of Oedipus by, 131–32

Gauguin, Paul, 141; *Jacob Wrestling with the Angel*, 141

Germany: attitude to the classics, 127–29, 169; scholarship of, 51; in twentieth century, 137, 150

Gnosis, 80–81

Goethe, J. W. von, 127–35 passim, 169; *Iphigenia in Tauris*, 127–35, 169

Graduate Schools, 51

Greece: culture of, 33, 36; drama of, 130–31; education of, 33–35; ideal of humanism in, 60, 62, 134–35; influence of, on Germany, 127–29; influence of, on Rome, 36–37, 68; poetry of, 149; politics of, 33, 35; studies of, compared with Roman, 148

Greek, language, 13, 36, 42

Gregory, the Great, Pope, 43

Haldane, Lord, 8

Harvard College, 47

Hellenistic Age, 35, 156; art of, 146, 158, 160; compared to twentieth century, 150; ideals of, expressed in *Aeneid*, 158–59, 160

Heresy, 74–75

Hölderlin, Friedrich, 128

Horace, 15, 17, 91–92, 151–53, 157; *Ars Poetica*, 15, 39; *Odes*, 26, 92, 151, 157; *Satires*, 92

Humanism, 3–27 passim, 53–54, 56–57, 58–70 passim, 75, 77, 98, 100–101, 103, 122–23, 123 n.1; Christian, 29, 47, 58–62, 65–66, 70, 79, 82–83, 85–86, 87, 95, 110; classical, xv, 46–49, 62–64, 94, 99, 105, 120, 121–22; in Jerome, 95–98, 120–23; in Lucretius, 153; New, 3, 4–5, 6, 11, 16, 17, 21, 23, 25, 172; pagan, 59, 66, 72, 78, 82, 86, 95, 109

Humanists, 10–11, 23, 56–57, 68, 75, 107, 109; classical, 16, 18, 19, 24; New, 26; Renaissance, xiv

Humanitas, 16, 38, 52, 67, 68, 72, 75, 79, 83, 92, 94

Humanities, 3, 11, 19, 21–22, 170, 171; classical, 15, 170

Ignatius of Loyola, Saint, 32–33, 41, 47, 53
Interdisciplinary studies, 22–23
Iphigenia, 130, 132–33. *See also* Goethe
Isocrates, 33–35, 37, 38; *Panegyricus*, 35

Jerome, Saint, 89–90, 94, 95–123 passim; attitude toward marriage of, 111, 113–14, 117, 118; character of, 97, 104, 116–19; and Christian humanism, 95–96, 103; as *Ciceronianus*, 120–23; education of, 98, 100; erudition of, 96–97, 97–101, 103, 117, 119, 120; misogyny of, 103–4; and the pagan classics, 95, 97–101, 103, 122; portraits of, 122; psychological eccentricity of, 104, 116–17, 118, 119, 120; reputation of, in Middle Ages, 95–97, 99–100, 101, 116, 119, 123; reputation of, in Renaissance, 97, 101; and rhetoric, 100–101, 109; as satirist, 101–4; uses of Scripture by, 110–16, 120; scurrility of, 104; shortcomings of, as humanist, 99–101, 101–2, 103, 104, 105, 120–23; shortcomings of, as theologian, 107; skill with words of, 96, 99, 101, 105–6, 110, 118–19, 120; style, 105–10; as translator, 105–7, 116; *Letters*, 89, 100, 110, 111, 112; *Lives of the Desert Fathers*, 62, 105; *Treatise against Jovinian*, 89, 98, 107, 111–14, 125 n.17; *Vulgate*, 96, 106

Jesuit: education, 31–33, 41; Order, 50

Kaufmann, R. J., 10–11, 17

Latin, 30, 36, 38, 40, 42, 43, 44, 46, 56, 68–69, 92–94, 105–6; barbaric, 43; and Christianity, 92–94, 105–10; Ciceronian, 42; Golden Age of, 68, 69, 109, 136, 150; medieval, 44; as medium of communication, 43, 44, 46, 48, 109; Silver age of, 41, 98; structure of, 69, 93, 107–8; vocabulary, changes in, 93–94, 106–7
Law: practice of, 40; Roman, 45; study of, 45, 48
Learning, revival of: Carolingian, 44; Renaissance, 47–48
Liberal Arts, 38, 48; colleges of, 31, 50
Lucretius, 153–56, 157, 167 n.36; influence on Vergil of, 160; *De Rerum Natura*, 150, 154, 157

Mann, Thomas, 137, 146, 164 n.10; *Doctor Faustus*, 137–38, 150, 155, 156
Matisse, Henri, 141, 142, 157, 159; *Dance*, 141; *Harmony in Red*, 141; *Music*, 141
Medicine, in medieval education, 45
Miller, Henry, 155, 165 n.24, 167 n.37; *Sexus*, 167 n.37; *Tropic of Cancer*, 165 n.24
Myth: Christian, 70–72, 85; classical, reworked, 129–30, 131–32; pagan, 81. 84–85; in Scripture, 82

Neo-Platonism, 71, 80, 140
New York, 142; as center of art, 139, 142–43; school of painting, 142, 143

Orestes, 132–33, 160
Ovid, 44, 46

Paris: as cultural center, 140, 142–43; decline of, in art, 139, 142
Philosophy: Christian, 74–77; in Ciceronian system, 37–38; ethical, 16; and faith, 75–76; Greek and Roman, 70–71; Hellenistic, 160; in Isocratean system, 34; in medieval education, 38, 45; pagan, 87
Picasso, Pablo, 139, 159, 161
Pindar, 33
Plato, 16, 34, 37, 45, 56, 73; influence of, on Vergil, 160; theory of Ideas of, 70
Pollock, Jackson, 139, 142, 159; *Blue Poles*, 139–40, 159
Porter, David, 18
Protestantism, 31, 32, 40
Putnam, Michael, 167 n.43

Quintilian, 33, 39, 40–42, 89; *Institutio Oratoria*, 33, 40–41, 43

Ratio Studiorum, 31–32, 41, 42, 53, 55
Reformation, 31
Renaissance, 29, 30, 46–48, 58, 59; education, 46–49; Italian, xiv
Renaissance man, 20, 121; classicists as, 21
Rhetoric, 33–35, 36–42, 100–

101; in the Fathers, 89–92; in Jerome, 100–101, 109
Rilke, Rainer Maria, 167 n.36
Roche, John P., 5
Rome: Augustan, 156, 160, 161; history of, 160; ideal of humanism in, 62; literary tradition of, 24, 42, 68–69, 88–89, 90–92; literature of, influence of, upon twentieth century, 136, 146–47, 150, 163; pessimistic view of, 167 n.43; philosophy and ethics of, 123 n.3; poetry of, 136, 138, 146, 149, 163; political life of, 37; religion of, 72–73; studies of, compared with Greek, 148; society of, 39–40, 103–4

Sade, Marquis de, 140–41
Satire: in Jerome, 101–4, 105; Roman, 101–2, 104
Science: and classics, 19, 21, 22–23, 28; Hellenistic, 160; and humanities, 21, 22
Scripture, 65, 73, 79, 96, 107, 110–16, 119; Jerome as translator of, 96, 105–7, 116; Jerome's uses of, 110–16
Sidonius, Bishop of Lyons, 43
Sophists, 33–34
Sophocles, 131; *Oedipus the King*, 131, 138. *See also* Freud
Stein, Gertrude, 142
Stevenson, Robert Louis, 141; *Dr. Jekyll and Mr. Hyde*, 141
Stravinsky, Igor, 141; *The Rite of Spring*, 141

Sturm, Johann, 31, 32
Syme, Sir Ronald, 148–49, 167 n.43; *The Roman Revolution*, 148, 156

Testament: Old, 63, 104, 112, 113; New, 63, 94, 113
Theology: and Christian dogma, 79–80; in medieval education, 45
Topoi, 90–91, 102, 103

Universities, medieval, 45

Vergil, 43, 63, 73, 143, 147, 156–60, 161, 162. *Aeneid*, 138, 147, 150, 158–60, 162;

Eclogues, 136, 157; *Georgics*, 157–58, 159. *See also* Aeneas, *Aeneid*
Vespasian, Emperor, 39–40, 41

Wilbur, Richard, 155, 166 n.36
Wilde, Oscar, 141–42; *The Picture of Dorian Grey*, 141–42
Winckelmann, Johann Joachim, 128–29
World War: First, 29, 49, 140, 142, 143; Second, 11, 13, 137, 148, 156

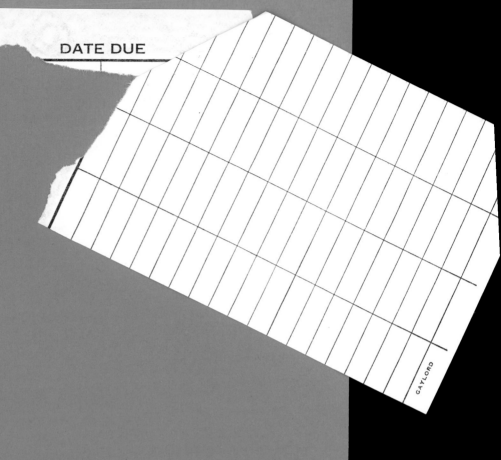